Computer Activities Across the Curriculum

Grades K–5

Editor
Emily R. Smith, M.A. Ed.

Editorial Project Manager
Elizabeth Morris, Ph. D.

Editor-in-Chief
Sharon Coan, M.S. Ed.

Cover Artist
Wendy Roy

Art Coordinator
Denice Adorno

Imaging
Alfred Lau
James Edward Grace
Temo Parra

Product Manager
Phil Garcia

Acknowledgements
Trademarks: Trademarked names and graphics appear throughout this book. Instead of listing every firm and entity which owns the trademarks or inserting a trademark symbol with each mention of a trademarked names, the publisher avers that it is using the names and graphics only for editorial purposes and to the benefit of the trademarked owner with no intention of infringing upon that trademark.

Publishers
Rachelle Cracchiolo, M.S. Ed.
Mary Dupuy Smith, M.S. Ed.

Authors
Michael R. Doub
Marianne C. Hicks
Bev Zee Ann Stevens
Heidi R. Stirm
Suzanne Y. Wilkinson

Lesson Contributors
Mountain View Elementary School
Colorado Springs, Colorado

Debbie Bonnett
Debi Boruff
Betty Flory
Melissa Foster
Nan Koehler
Lethia Lee
Beth Marr
Gayle Nyquist

Lisa Padgett
Eva Pokorny
Cris Robirds
Jan Strycker
Kerry Trietley
Anne Warren
Jane Williams

Teacher Created Materials, Inc.
6421 Industry Way
Westminster, CA 92683
www.teachercreated.com
ISBN-0-7439-3032-0
©2001 Teacher Created Materials, Inc.
Reprinted, 2004
Made in U.S.A.

Table of Contents

Table of Contents *(cont.)*

Introduction

Over the next few pages are some management ideas for how to successfully integrate technology into the elementary classroom. At Mountain View Elementary School, we feel that the first step to using technology is to work with the professionals in the school to set up the following foundations:

- a technology philosophy statement

- a schoolwide plan for classroom management of technology

- sample computer menus for teachers to use as models

- example computer rotation schedules

- plans for maintaining the equipment

- a firm plan of action for handling vital technology issues

Technology Philosophy Statement

A few years ago, our staff wrote our technology philosophy statement. It is now posted around the school and by all of our computer stations. We feel this statement is as important to the success of our students as the district and state philosophy statements. We have separate statements for our general school philosophy and our technology philosophy. Some schools have, instead, chosen to alter their current school philosophy statement to include technology.

Sample Technology Philosophy Statement

- Technology is an integral part of the learning process. It is a tool used in the learning environment throughout all curricular areas to help teach written and oral communication skills, problem identification, and critical-thinking skills.

- Students and staff integrate technology to the fullest extent for accessing, processing, and analyzing information.

- Technology is used to promote academic success by empowering students to become creative problem solvers as well as self-paced learners.

Classroom Management of Technology

Following are some possible technology management techniques. Though each class differs in its methods, this will give teachers an idea of managing technology in the classroom. To further define procedures, we have separated the procedures by primary and intermediate levels.

Primary (K–2)

In one all-day kindergarten classroom, there are seven computers grouped together in a rectangular-shaped center. Center time is scheduled for both morning and afternoon sessions. During center time, computers are usually a free choice for students. The activities on the computer are guided by the software that is curriculum related (chosen by the teacher). This center time is a 30-minute period, and students are allowed to migrate among centers as space permits. When there are not enough computers for each student to use, students may work with partners. If a particular activity has been assigned, an alphabetical class list of first names is posted. Students mark off their names when they have completed the activity.

In grades 1–2, groups rotate through the computers during math centers. The groups are chosen by the tables where the students sit to do their seatwork. Tables are called for 10- to 15-minute rotations, while other students are doing different math activities. If time allows, all students have an opportunity for computer work during one session. If there is limited time, the schedule is carried over to the next day's math time, thus assuring that each student has a computer on which to work within a two-day period.

In one first grade classroom, we are very fortunate to have eight computers. Three of these computers have internal CD-ROMs and monitors large enough to run most any CD program. The computers are set up on countertops arranged along two opposite walls in the room. During our 90 minutes of center time each morning, the students have three different 30-minute sessions through which they rotate: learning centers, teacher center, and computers. During their computer time each week, a rotation schedule is posted to give each student a chance to use one of the larger machines (PowerMacs) to complete an assignment. This schedule also gives each student a chance to use a different type of machine during a two-week period. The students generally work at the machines on an individual basis, but they are free to seek assistance from each other as well.

Classroom Management of Technology *(cont.)*

Intermediate (3–5)

Although there is no guarantee that all the students will get exactly the same amount of time on the computers, we do our best with the scheduling. Many intermediate teachers have a computer rotation schedule that allows the students to be on the computers for a set amount of time (see example on page 7). The students rotate morning and afternoon, and also from day to day. One guideline to scheduling is that students are not on computers when there is a guest speaker, during tests, during special events, or during assemblies. They understand this and realize that we do our best to give them equal time, but sometimes this does not occur. If students are absent, we try to allow them to stay in at recess or come in before or after school to make up the time. While the students are on computer rotation, they complete the assignments on the Computer Menu (see example on page 8). These usually contain short-term assignments, such as sending e-mail or working on the Internet, as well as long-term assignments, such as CD-ROM research and multimedia projects. In our classes, the Computer Menu is changed every two weeks.

Maintenance

As with classroom management techniques, maintenance of hardware, software, and schedules is established on an individual classroom basis. Generally speaking, primary student responsibilities are fewer than those of intermediate students. In a fifth grade classroom, all technology supplies (i.e., CD-ROMs, headphones, Classroom Technology Notebooks) are kept in one section of the classroom. The students get the supplies as needed. It is usually necessary, however, to have a student monitor check the area at the end of the day.

Students use headphones when on the computer so the sounds do not disrupt the rest of the class. When done, the students wipe the headphones with sterile pads to keep the headphones clean. CD-ROMs or disks are replaced in correct packaging and returned to their storage areas.

The Classroom Technology Notebook has copies of all Computer Menus, examples of assignments, step-by-step instructions for some technology skills, and all Internet assignments.

Example Computer Rotation Schedule

	Day 1	**Day 2**	**Day 3**
A.M.	Brian	Lauren	Matt
A.M.	Jasmine	Jamal	Jimmy
A.M.	Amy	Bryan	Kyle
A.M.	Sally	Byron	Sylvia
A.M.	Joey	Kelsey	Ollie
Lunch	Lunch	Lunch	Lunch
P.M.	Mackenzie	Phu	Kenny
P.M.	Kim	Brittany	Emmett
P.M.	Darcy	Olivia	Tiffany
P.M.	Chris	Timothy	Jill
P.M.	Shane	Teri	Rachel

Sample Computer Menu

Make sure all previous assignments have been completed.

- *HyperStudio*—Your limerick is overdue! It needs to be complete with limerick, background, and buttons to link to a title page.

- **E-mail**—Answer your new e-mail assignment! Make sure your answers are in complete sentences.

- *ClarisWorks Draw*—Create angles with the following measurements: 90°, 38°, 115°, 145°, 180°, and 67°. Label the measurements telling whether they are acute, obtuse, or right angles. Also, using any of the following measurements, create scalene, isosceles, right, and equilateral triangles—6 cm, 5 cm, and 4 cm. Label your triangles correctly. Don't forget—always use a plastic protractor on the computer screen!

- *Treasure Island* **CD-ROM**—Chapter 8, "At the Sign of the Spy Glass"

  1. What made Long-John Silver different from other buccaneers?
  2. Write three sentences describing Long-John Silver's appearance.
  3. On page 157, Long-John Silver asks Morgan what he and Black Dog were "jawing" about. What does this mean?
  4. What is Long-John Silver's "score"?
  5. Define the following terms:

     - seafaring–p. 151
     - anecdote–p. 162
     - quid–p. 156
     - threshold–p. 154
     - dexterity–p. 152
     - swab–p. 156

- **Internet**—Complete the Internet assignment, Earth Viewer. Don't forget that this is due next week.

Considerations for Implementing Technology

This is a list of issues schools should consider regarding the implementation of technology. Some of these issues are ongoing and need to be reviewed on an annual basis.

Issues to consider when first implementing technology

- What are the school's goals for technology (norms)?
  - administration's goals
  - technology support person's goals
  - classroom teachers' goals
- What is the technology specialist's role—All teaching? Lab specialist? Troubleshooter? Combination of all three?
- What type of funding will be available for implementation of technology?
- What types of staff development will be available for teachers?
- What types of hardware, including peripheral hardware (scanners, DVD players, VCRs, digital cameras, etc.), will the school be purchasing and using?
- What types of software will the teachers integrate into the curriculum (CD-ROMs, multimedia, creativity software, skill and drill, etc.)?
- Where will computers/multimedia station components be placed (lab, classroom, or combination)?
- What are the school's power sources? Where are the power sources located?
- What kind of surge protection will the school have (internal to building)?
- What kind of network system will the school have (internal, external, hub locations, runs from server, switches, etc.)?
- What kind of furniture will be used with the equipment (ergonomic considerations: chairs, counters at appropriate heights for different age groups, book holders, etc.)?
- What will be the school's five-year plan for curricular area integration? (Possibly concentrate on one curricular area per year.)
- What plan will teachers/administrators have for a home-to-school connection?
- What kind of Internet access will the students have? (Develop a purpose for use, firewall, and get permission from parents for usage.)

Considerations for Implementing Technology *(cont.)*

Issues to consider when first implementing technology *(cont.)*

- How will classes address ethics with technology (copyright issues, respecting other students' files, etc.)?

- What will be the internal purpose for the school Web site? Will it be for general information only? Will teachers and/or students create it? Will it be set up for parents to access homework?

- Do the school's goals coordinate with district goals and align with state standards?

- Will the staff provide maintenance for the equipment? How will district contracts/support affect the school's goals?

Issues to consider annually

- What are the school's goals for technology (norms)?

  - administration's goals
  - technology support person's goals
  - classroom teachers' goals

- What types of hardware, including peripheral hardware (scanners, DVD players, VCRs, digital cameras, etc.), will the school be purchasing and using?

- What types of software will teachers integrate into the curriculum (CD-ROMs, multimedia, creativity software, skill and drill, etc.)?

- What type of funding will be available for implementation of technology?

- What types of staff development will be available for teachers?

- What plan will teachers/administrators have for a home-to-school connection?

- What kind of Internet access will the students have? (Develop a purpose for use, firewall, and get permission from parents for usage.)

- What will be the internal purpose for the school Web site? Will it be for general information only? Will teachers and/or students create it? Will it be set up for parents to access homework?

- Do the school's goals coordinate with district goals and align with state standards?

- Will the staff provide maintenance for the school's equipment? How will district contracts/support affect the school's goals?

Alphabet Books

Objectives

In this activity, students will

- draw a letter and picture to match the beginning sound of that letter.
- use letter stamps and picture stamps to illustrate the sound.
- print pictures with teacher assistance.

Technology required

- *Kid Pix* or other graphics program
- printer

Materials needed

- copies of *What Do You Hear in the ABC's?* (page 12) for the students

Description

Students will use *Kid Pix* or another graphics program to draw each letter and then either draw a picture or use a "stamp" that corresponds to the sound of the letter. Have students either individually complete pictures for all the letters of the alphabet or work in groups to make an ABC book for the letter sounds. Before moving to the computers, they can use *What Do You Hear in the ABC's?* (page 12) to brainstorm words for the letters.

If the students will be drawing the letters, the teacher needs to demonstrate how to use the drawing tools to make letters and pictures. If the students will be using stamps, demonstrate how to use the letter and picture stamps. If the class is using *Kid Pix*, be sure to show students how to hold the option and shift keys down at the same time so the picture can be enlarged.

Show students how to print their work in color or black and white. Students or groups can then print their letters and make alphabet books of their work.

Extension

Students can make covers for their alphabet books by stamping all the ABC's on a title page in a creative manner. Students can also make other ABC books for subjects being covered in class.

Name _____

What Do You Hear in the ABC's?

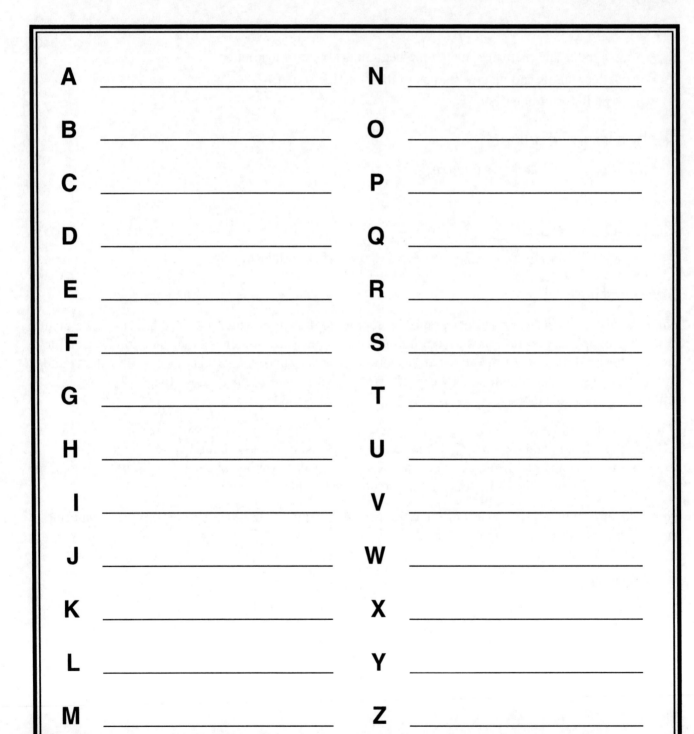

A	_____	N	_____
B	_____	O	_____
C	_____	P	_____
D	_____	Q	_____
E	_____	R	_____
F	_____	S	_____
G	_____	T	_____
H	_____	U	_____
I	_____	V	_____
J	_____	W	_____
K	_____	X	_____
L	_____	Y	_____
M	_____	Z	_____

12

Card Making

Objective

In this activity, students will

- use the card maker program to design and print cards for special occasions.

Technology required

- *Bailey's Book House* or other card maker program
- printer

Materials needed

- copies of *Designing a Card* (page 14) for the students

Description

Have students use *Designing a Card* (page 14) to plan their cards before they go to the computer.

Demonstrate special features of the card maker program the students are using. Show the students how to pick the card style and design the card. Most programs feature a variety of holiday, invitation, and miscellaneous choices. Students can also use word processing programs to design cards, but using word processing will probably require more teacher assistance.

As students create their cards, tell them to make sure their spelling is accurate and graphics are appropriate for the particular occasion. Once the cards are completed, have students print their cards. Students can add color to the cards if the class does not have a color printer.

Extension

After students have made one card, allow them to work independently to make other cards for special occasions such as Mother's Day or Earth Day.

Name _____

Designing a Card

Directions: Use this activity sheet to design your card.

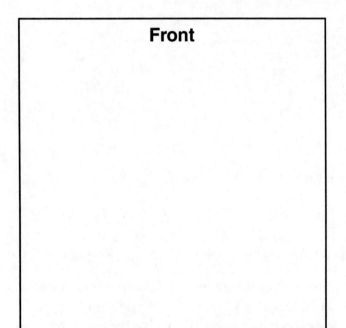

Front

Back

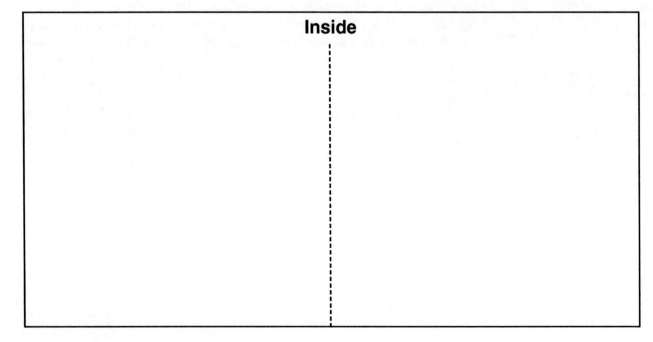

Inside

I'm an Artist

Objectives

In this activity, students will

- draw their favorite animals using colored pencils.
- orally present who they are, what animal they drew, and what are their favorite things to do in school.

Technology required

- *Kid Pix* or other slide show program
- scanner

Materials needed

- paper
- colored pencils
- copies of *What Are You Going to Say?* (page 16) for the students

Description

First, have the students draw their favorite animals using colored pencils. Then bring the students up to the scanner in small groups (maybe base the groups on the type of animals they drew). Demonstrate how to use the scanner and then assist the students in scanning their pictures. If the school doesn't have a scanner, have the students draw the animals in a draw program rather than scanning them.

Using a slide show program, work with the small groups to create a slide show of their drawings. So, the class might have slide shows with the following titles: Mammals, Fish, Amphibians, etc.

Finally, have a sharing day where the students' pictures are projected as each student gets up, introduces him/herself, talks about his/her favorite things to do in school, and his/her animal picture. Students can use *What Are You Going to Say?* (page 16) to prepare their brief presentations.

Extension

Have students design short slide shows about their favorite animals. The slides can include information about where the animals live, what they eat, and why the students like them.

Name _____

What Are You Going to Say?

Your Name _____

Your Animal _____

What you like to do in school_____

_____

_____

_____

_____

_____

_____

_____

Letter Machine

Objective

In this activity, students will

- identify letters on the ABC keyboard or choose random letters to identify by clicking on the letters' symbols.

Technology required

- *Bailey's Book House*

Materials needed

- none

Description

This activity is probably most appropriate for kindergarten students. Use this activity to introduce sounds for letters or as reinforcement for letter identification.

First, demonstrate the letter machine program. Students will see how to click on the letter of their choice to hear the name of that letter along with a sound jingle demonstrating the sound letter relationship. For example: Z is a picture of a zebra zipping to make the zipper sound.

Then allow each student to click on letters at his/her own pace. After students have gotten to know the program, ask them to click on specific letters to test their letter identification ability.

Extension

This program can be used with any pre-reader who already knows the letters and is ready to identify sounds.

If the students are ready, have them make their own letter machine program using a slide show program. Each slide could be a large stamp of the letter of the alphabet. Then, students can record the sound for each letter and have it play when the slide show is running.

Name Books

Objective

In this activity, students will

- associate the letters of their names with other items that begin with the same letters.

Technology required

- *Stanley's Sticker Stories*
- *Microsoft Word, AppleWorks,* or other word processing program

Materials needed

- copies of *Who Are You?* (page 19) for the students

Description

As beginning readers learn to associate the letters in their names with other words, have them keep lists of words that start with the various letters in their names. For example: Jacob would find words that begin with j, a, c, o, and b. Students can use *Who Are You?* (page 19) to keep track of their possible descriptive words.

Assign students the task of creating name books for themselves. Each page represents a different letter in their names. In the *Stanley's Sticker Stories* program, students type a sentence like "J is for jack-o-lantern." They then find other pictures in the program that start with those same letters and put them on the page. In a word processing program, students type the sentence and change the font and style to fill the page. Then, students use clip art to decorate the page.

Students can add their voices to each "page" to tell about the page. The book can then be "played" on the computer or printed out. Consider printing them in color and binding them together into a book for each student.

Extension

The same program can be used for a variety of book-writing activities at higher levels.

Name _____

Who Are You?

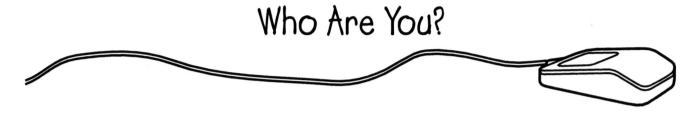

Directions: Use this sheet to keep track of words that describe you. Write your name in the boxes, one letter per box. Then, write words that begin with the letters of your name on each of the lines. Try to think of as many words as you can.

Name Stamping

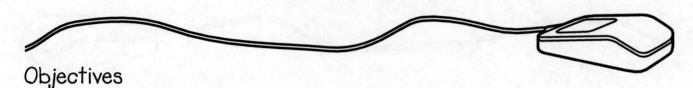

Objectives

In this activity, students will

- stamp their first names using letter stamps.
- decorate their names using at least five different picture stamps.
- print pictures with teacher assistance.

Technology required

- *Kid Pix* or other graphics program
- printer

Materials needed

- none

Description

Using a graphics program, demonstrate for the students how to stamp, type, or paint words. Then have the students stamp, type, or paint each letter from their names.

Once the name is completed, have each student find five or more object stamps that begin with the same letters as the letters in their names. Then, students use the stamps to place the decorations around their stamped names. Finally, have the students use the pencil tool to write how each picture relates to them. See the example on page 21.

Have students print their name pictures. After the pictures are printed, students can color them (if the students didn't print them in color), cut out the name design, and frame them by pasting them onto pieces of colored construction paper.

Extension

Students can decorate both their first and their last names. Allow students to change the size of the print.

Name Stamping Example

Nursery Rhymes

Objectives

In this activity, students will

- use the drawing tool to illustrate nursery rhymes.
- print pictures with teacher assistance.

Technology required

- *Kid Pix* or other graphics program
- printer

Materials needed

- copies of nursery rhymes
- copies of *Nursery Rhyme Art* (page 23) for the students

Description

Begin this lesson by sharing several nursery rhymes with the students. Using a graphics program, students will be illustrating their favorite nursery rhymes. Before having the students go to the computer, have them plan their drawings on *Nursery Rhyme Art* (page 23). The planning sheet has a place for each student to write the nursery rhyme and a place for a sketch of the picture. Remind students to write the names and authors (if known) of the nursery rhymes they are using.

Demonstrate how to use the drawing tools to illustrate the nursery rhymes the students have heard. Have students type or stamp the title and/or text of the nursery rhymes to the left of their drawings.

Once the pictures are complete, have the students print their masterpieces and color them (if the students printed in black and white).

Extension

Have students illustrate a number of nursery rhymes this way and make their own nursery rhyme collection books.

Name _____

Nursery Rhyme Art

Drawing

Writing

Title _____

Author _____

Buddy Biographies

Objectives

In this activity, students will

- write biographies about their primary buddies.
- write autobiographies about themselves.
- create a multimedia class project.

Technology required

- *PowerPoint*, *HyperStudio*, *Scene Slate*, or another multimedia program

Materials needed

- copies of *All About You* (page 25) for the students
- copies of *All About Me* (page 26) for the students

Description

This project will take place over a few weeks, depending upon the schedules of the two classes involved. You will need to find a primary teacher who is willing to have his/her students be buddies with your class. Assign each student a designated buddy that he/she will pair up with for the activities.

First, they need to complete the two activity pages *All About You* (page 25) and *All About Me* (page 26) together so that the older student can include this information about themselves and the primary buddies. Then, students create scenes about themselves and their buddies. The upper graders should probably do much of the typing in order to use the computer lab time efficiently. The primary students can help with the mouse manipulation. Then students can select the pictures and backgrounds together.

When all the students are finished with their individual projects, be sure to have all the pairs share their masterpieces. The students, teachers, and parents will love it. It's a great collaborative project!

Extension

Students can extend this activity by reading biographies or autobiographies about famous people for a reading unit.

Names _____

All About You

Directions: Use this activity page to record the answers as you interview your primary buddy. Let your buddy use the space on the right of your written answers to draw pictures to describe his/her answers.

When were you born (month, day, and year)?

_____

Where were you born (city, state, and/or country)?

_____

Tell me five special things about yourself.

- • _____

- • _____

- • _____

- • _____

- • _____

What is your favorite thing about school?

_____

_____

_____

Tell me about your family.

_____

_____

_____

Names_____

All About Me

Directions: As your primary buddy draws pictures to describe his/her answers, fill out the spaces below with the answers to the following questions.

Date of birth (month, day, and year): _____

Place of birth (city, state, and country): _____

Five unique things about me:

- _____
- _____
- _____
- _____
- _____

Favorite thing about school: _____

Least favorite thing about school: _____

Description of my family:_____

_____

_____

Description of what I want to be when I grow up: _____

_____

_____

_____

What I like about my little buddy: _____

_____

_____

Choose Your Own Adventure

Objectives

In this activity, students will

- write their own adventure stories.
- turn their stories into multimedia presentations.

Technology required

- *PowerPoint, HyperStudio, Scene Slate,* or another multimedia program
- graphics for the students to use in their slides/scenes/cards

Materials needed

- copies of *Adventure Story Planning Sheet* (page 28) for the students
- copy of a *Choose Your Own Adventure* book

Description

To begin this lesson, read *Choose Your Own Adventure* stories to the students. Outline the basic project requirements and introduce the software. Students need to plan stories that will follow a general story line but give viewers various options created by the students.

Students need to plan their stories along multiple story lines using the *Adventure Story Planning Sheet* (page 28).

Once the planning stage is completed, students can begin designing their stories on the computer. Students need to create a scene for each choice in their stories. Graphics should be added only after the complete story with all of its choices is done. Be sure that students review their stories to ensure that all the links have been made correctly and that navigating through their stories is easy.

Extension

Stories can be expanded length-wise, graphics added, or the project can be expanded to a full-blown multimedia extravaganza.

Name _____

Adventure Story Planning Sheet

Title Card	
Choice 3	
Choice 3c	
Choice 3a	
Choice 3b	
Choice 2	
Choice 2a	
Choice 2c	
Choice 2b	
Choice 1	
Choice 1c	
Choice 1a	
Choice 1b	

Creative Class Web Sites

Objective

In this activity, students will

- work in groups to create different sections of a class Web site.

Technology required

- *PageMill* or other Web design software
- Internet connection
- digital camera or 35mm camera and scanner

Materials needed

- copies of *Web Site Flow Chart* (page 30) for the students
- overhead transparency of *Flow Chart Example* (page 31)

Description

Begin by holding a brainstorming session in which the class shares all their ideas about what they want the Web site to look like. Then, divide the students into groups and allow them to decide which subject area they would like to design with their partners. Have them begin their designing by completing the *Web Site Flow Chart* (page 30). The teacher may want to review flow charts by sharing the *Flow Chart Example* (page 31).

Once the flow charts are approved by the teacher, students can start writing their articles about what they're studying in class. They may also take pictures with the digital camera or scan pictures into their projects. When their articles are approved, they may start typing them into *PageMill* or another Web page design software program.

After the various sections are done, which takes time, talk to the school's technology specialist to see how to upload the information onto the school's Web site. The students should update their sections each month. Set up the process so that the teacher approves student writing before it appears on the Web site.

Extension

Students can extend their research to compare and contrast their Web page to other schools' Web pages. They can also learn how to import sound, moving video, and animated graphics to enhance their pages.

Name _____

Web Site Flow Chart

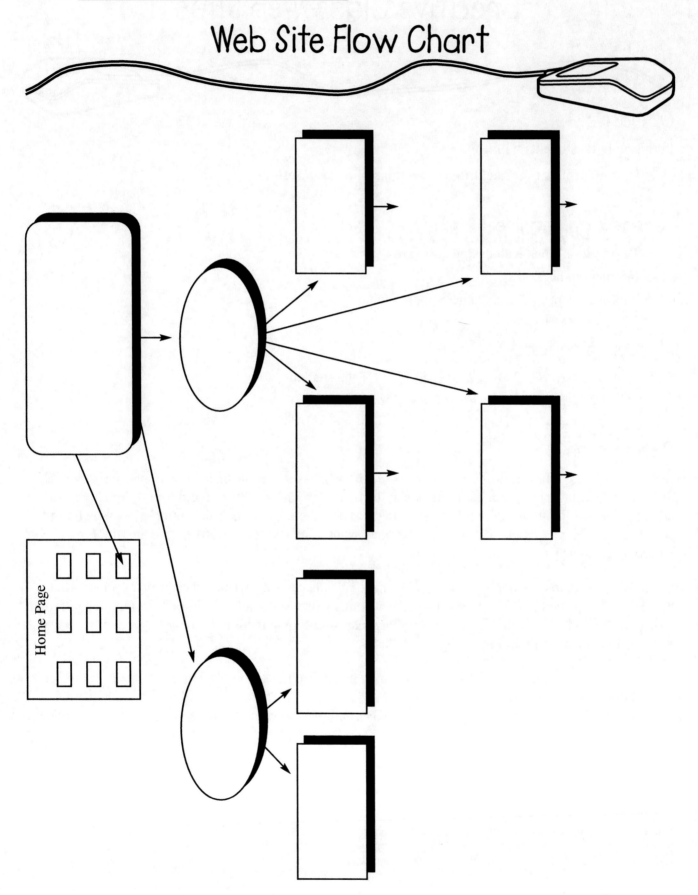

Home Page

Flow Chart Example

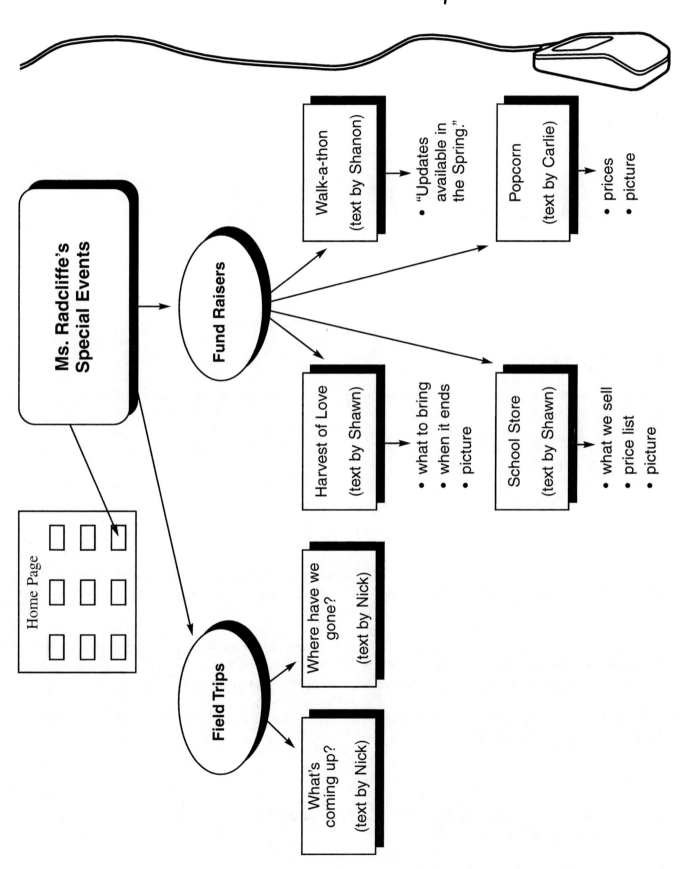

Daily Briefing

Objectives

In this activity, students will

- improve their abilities to listen for meaning.
- summarize a radio news clip.

Technology required

- *Microsoft Word, AppleWorks,* or other word processing program
- Internet connection

Materials needed

- copies of *Daily Briefing Notepad* (page 33) for the students

Description

This can be used as a daily assignment—done independently after initial instruction at the beginning of the year.

Demonstrate for students how to access the *Earth and Sky* Web site through the *Teacher Created Materials* Web site for this book:

> Go to **http://www.teachercreated.com/books/3032**
>
> Click on Page 33, Site 1

Once on the *Earth and Sky* Web site, click on **Today's Show**. A new page will appear with a written transcript of the show, a graphic to support the information, and a button for accessing the show via RealPlayer.

Direct the students to listen to (or read aloud) the radio clip twice, focusing on the main idea and one or two supporting details. The objective is for them to improve their ability to listen for meaning, retain the information, and then take notes on the *Daily Briefing Notepad* (page 33).

After listening, have the students write a short paragraph about the news brief. Then review the short paragraphs at the end of the day.

Extension

Require listeners to add more supporting details to their notes. Have them listen to more than one news brief or listen to more challenging briefs.

Name _____

Daily Briefing Notepad

Access the *Earth and Sky* Web site:

Go to **http://www.teachercreated.com/books/3032**

Click on Page 33, Site 1

Once on the *Earth and Sky* Web site, click on **Today's Show**. A new page will appear with a written transcript of the show, a graphic to support the information, and a button for accessing the show via RealPlayer.

Listen to (or read aloud) the radio clip twice, focusing on the main idea and one or two supporting details. As you listen, use this page to take notes. After completing this page, write a paragraph about the news brief.

Today's Date _____

Title of News Brief _____

Topic of News Brief _____

What is the main idea covered in Today's Show?

_____

_____

_____

What are two supporting ideas shared on the show?

_____

_____

Go van Gogh!

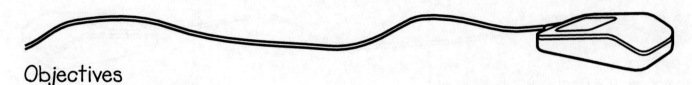

Objectives

In this activity, students will

- be introduced to the life and work of Vincent van Gogh.
- review the concept that artists have certain styles to their paintings.
- review what warm and cool colors are.

Technology required

- Internet connection

Materials needed

- copies of *Art History Appreciation Lesson* (page 35) for the students
- copies of pictures by Vincent van Gogh
- books about Vincent van Gogh

Description

Read a book about van Gogh (like *Getting to Know the World's Greatest Artists—van Gogh* by Mike Venezia) and look at posters and/or calendar pictures of van Gogh's artwork.

Demonstrate how to access the *WebMuseum, Paris* Web site through the *Teacher Created Materials* Web site for this book:

       Go to **http://www.teachercreated.com/books/3032**

       Click on Page 35, Site 1

Introduce the students to the *WebMuseum, Paris* site on van Gogh and go over the questions on the *Art History Appreciation Lesson* (page 35) activity page. The students can then work on the computers independently and turn in their answer sheets when completed.

Extension

Have the students complete research on other artists. They can then compare the work of those painters with Vincent van Gogh's work.

Name _____

Art History Appreciation Lesson

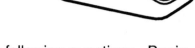

Directions: Read the *WebMuseum, Paris* Web site to answer the following questions. Begin by accessing the *WebMuseum* Web site:

Go to **http://www.teachercreated.com/books/3032**

Click on Page 35, Site 1

1. Click on the two subject matter areas (i.e., portraits, irises, other landscapes) to view more pictures. Which two areas did you choose and why did you choose those two areas?

   _____

   _____

   _____

2. Click on two paintings to make them larger and observe van Gogh's style. What are two things that make van Gogh's paintings different from other paintings you have seen?

   _____

   _____

3. Look at the colors in van Gogh's paintings. Find two pictures—one with warm color dominance and one that is mainly in cool colors. Which paintings did you choose?

   • warm color dominance _____

   • cool color dominance _____

4. What is your favorite work of art by Vincent van Gogh?

   _____

5. What is one new piece of information you learned about Vincent van Gogh from this site?

   _____

   _____

My Favorite Place to Read

Objective

In this activity, students will

- become acquainted with their classmates by sharing their favorite places to read.

Technology required

- any graphics program or desktop publishing program
- digital camera
- printer

Materials needed

- construction paper
- glue

Description

This lesson is a great activity to complete at the beginning of the school year to help students become acquainted with one another, to help the teacher learn more about each student's level of interest in reading, and to motivate all students to enjoy reading.

First, the teacher should share his/her love of reading and tell about his/her favorite place to curl up and read. Students then participate in an informal class discussion where they share their own favorite places to read good books. Students will most likely also discuss what some of their favorite books are. For homework that evening, have each student draw a picture of his/her favorite place to read. On the following day, students can again share information about where they enjoy reading.

Have students take digital pictures of each other. Demonstrate for the class how to download the pictures to a drawing or desktop publishing file. Students can then open new files and either scan their drawings from home into the computer or redraw their pictures in a graphics program. Then, students download the pictures of themselves and place themselves into their pictures of where they like to read. Students can, of course, add any extra graphics to the drawings to make them unique.

Have students print their one-page pictures and glue them on colored construction paper. Display these posters with the students' names to help them get to know each other.

Extension

Students can make a multimedia presentation about their favorite hobbies. Students can also have someone take digital pictures of themselves in their favorite places to read.

My Shoe

Objectives

In this activity, students will

- describe and write about their shoes.
- paste a picture of their shoes into a word processing document.

Technology required

- *Microsoft Word, AppleWorks*, or other word processing program
- *Kid Pix* or other graphics program
- printer

Materials needed

- shoes (the shoes can be whichever ones students happen to wear to school that day)

Description

This lesson is designed to give students a fun topic to confidently write about early in the school year. It can be used during the first week of school after summer vacation. Have students sit in a circle on the floor. Each student needs to toss one shoe (they usually have new shoes they are proud of) into the center of the circle. They should leave the matching shoes somewhere else in the room (not at their own desks). Mix up the shoes so that they end up in a big jumble.

Now, go around the circle, and have students describe their shoes using only three adjectives. After the third adjective, each student can call on someone to try to pick out the correct shoe. After allowing many students to describe their shoes with adjectives, switch the game. Next, students must take turns telling about one special place their shoes have been, possibly a recent vacation site. Again, they then pick a friend in the class to try to pick out the correct shoe.

Finally, have students compose stories from the point of view of their shoes. The stories should be about somewhere that the shoes have been recently. Have the students type their stories directly into the computers, print them, edit them offline, and then make the necessary corrections. Using *Kid Pix*, or some other graphics program, have students draw pictures of their shoes at the setting of their stories. Copy and paste the pictures into the word processing documents. Place the pictures attractively in the stories and print the document. Post the stories for everyone to enjoy.

Extension

Using ink and/or colored pencils, have students make life-size drawings of their shoes.

Publishing a Story

Objectives

In this activity, students will

- publish a writing project in a quick and easy way.

Technology required

- *Microsoft Word, AppleWorks*, or other word processing program
- graphics to place in the stories
- scanner
- printer

Materials needed

- none

Description

Teachers should have their students write stories and work through the writing process before completing this activity. This technology project is the final step in the writing process—publishing.

Before beginning, write a sample story and format it in the way that the students' finished projects should appear. Teachers should decide which technology elements must be included for their classes. Some suggestions include a scanned or downloaded image or drawing, a page border, special fonts, and color highlights (if there is a color printer in the classroom). Save this sample as a template by saving it as "stationery" in the word processing program. An example story is shown on page 39. Teachers may choose to use the example story from this book rather than producing their own.

Be sure the students have gone through the whole writing process before proceeding to the next step.

After finishing the story, students need to locate graphics (i.e., clip art, scanned image, downloaded Internet image) that complement their stories. Students then open the teacher-created template to create their published story (or look at a printed copy of the sample). When students open the template, they will actually be opening a copy. They will each replace the teachers' story with their own and add the appropriate illustration. Then, just like that, they have a polished story to print and share.

Extension

Allow students to change the font, style, and size of the text of their stories. Students could also insert multiple pictures to illustrate their stories.

Teacher Template Example

Like many Americans, my family spent a couple of weeks each summer cruising across the country in our huge station wagon, stopping to enjoy the attractions on the way. Our budget and our curiosity led us to many national parks during these annual trips. Some of the best memories of my youth revolve around the wonders we experienced at one park or another.

I've timed the geysers of **Yellowstone**, camped among the mountains of **Yosemite**, squinted up at **Mount Rushmore,** and hiked the **Grand Canyon**. But these activities are all tainted now, and the past will never seem quite so rosy. See, I experienced all of these things before the arrival of one of the greatest inventions: the Passport to Our National Parks.

If you are one of the millions of Americans unfamiliar with the Passport, you're probably wondering why I consider this to be one of the great modern innovations.

The Passport is a small blue binder, sold for about $6.00 at every national park site. (But it is so much more than that.) Inside, color coded and accompanied by detailed maps and illustrations, is a listing of every national park in the country (more than 500). The site information is cleverly divided by region, so you can quickly find out what national treasures await you in the Philadelphia city limits, or the Blue Ridge Mountains, or the Pacific Northwest. Additionally, the section for each region contains blank pages where you can keep a record of your visits to the various locations.

That's right, you can keep a permanent record of each of your visits to one of America's national parks. The information desk at each site is equipped with an ink pad and a stamp that you can use to record the date and the name of the park

in your book, for posterity. Each page fits four of these stamps, so there is plenty of room to collect these inky souvenirs and document your interest in our nation's past and present.

The Passport celebrates one of our great American traits—a love of our history, and a patriotic desire to cultivate and revisit the sites of our national triumphs.

Sliders

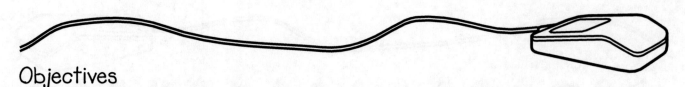

Objectives

In this activity, students will

- research topics and record organized information.
- write fictional stories incorporating factual research.
- include major story elements in their stories (setting, characterization, and plot).
- transcribe the stories into storyboard form.
- create slide shows to present their stories.

Technology required

- *Kid Pix* or other slide show program
- *Microsoft Word, AppleWorks*, or other word processing program
- scanner
- graphics to be added to the stories

Materials needed

- research materials
- copies of *Story Elements Map* (page 42) for the students
- copies of *Multimedia/Slide Show Planning Sheet* (page 43) for the students
- copies of fictional stories that incorporate research

Description

Begin this activity by holding a class discussion about fictional books that are based on research. Read aloud excerpts from several examples of books that incorporate researched information into a fictional story. Books by Joanne Ryder are excellent examples.

Either have each student choose a topic of interest to research or assign topics that relate to a current unit of study. Then, teach students how to organize and record the information they learn through research. Prior to researching, have them determine a specific number of questions to answer. For example: The questions for an animal might be some of these. What does it look like? What does it eat? Is it predator or prey? Where does it live? How does it move? Does it live alone or in groups? How does it care for its young?

Sliders *(cont.)*

Conduct lessons on the story elements of setting, characterization, and plot. Students can then begin planning and creating their fictional stories. Have students use the graphic organizer on the *Story Elements Map* (page 42) to organize their ideas. Students first draft their stories, then revise them. To help make sure they've included all the elements, have them use colored pencils to underline where they've included the various elements.

Once the stories are completed, have students divide their stories into sections. Each section will be one slide of his/her slide show. Students should draft illustrations for each slide on the *Multimedia/Slide Show Planning Sheet* (page 43). Students can include graphics (i.e., clip art, scanned images, downloaded images) in their slide shows. Once their stories have been storyboarded with all illustrations, clip art, and scanned pictures noted, they can begin creating their slides.

Students type each section of their stories and create slides by designing the backgrounds and pasting and placing text and importing graphics. The average slide show for this project is six to eight slides, including a title slide and a closing slide which has the bibliography of sources.

Have students pick transitions for their slides. Then let the students show their slide shows to family and friends.

Extension

Have students record themselves reading the text for each slide. Other sound effects can be selected and added, especially to the opening and closing slides.

Name _____

Story Elements Map

Directions: Use this map to record the different parts of your story. Be sure to indicate specific places where your research has influenced your authoring decisions.

Setting (where and when)

Characters

Conflict

Action/Events

Resolution

Name _____

Multimedia/Slide Show Planning Sheet

Title: _____

Slide # _____

Slide # _____

Slide # _____

Slide # _____

Slide # _____

Slide # _____

Surfing the Spider's Web

Objectives

In this activity, students will

- access selected Web sites and complete the given tasks for each.
- enter Web addresses, click on multiple links, scroll down, read from the screen, and print screens.

Technology required

- Internet connection

Materials needed

- copies of *The Spider's Web* (pages 46–47) for the students
- bulletin board of a large spider's web made out of black yarn
- large spider copied onto black construction paper—place on the bulletin board web (spider outline provided on page 48)
- nine book outlines with Web sites and tasks written on them posted on construction paper (book outline on page 49)
- one copy of the paper fly outline for each student (fly outlines on page 50)

Description

This is a great independent technology activity that students could complete using a center in the classroom. Using the outlines provided, put up a bulletin board with a spider in the center of a large web. Moving from the outside in, place book outlines on the web with a Web site address and task on each of them.

The students are directed to start at the outside of the web and work their way into the middle. At each Web site they open, they have to complete the given task. Before allowing the students to work on this activity, give students copies of *The Spider's Web* (pages 46–47) and look over the tasks together. Then, demonstrate the procedure for them.

Surfing the Spider's Web *(cont.)*

Demonstrate how to access each Web page through the *Teacher Created Materials* Web site for this book:

> Go to **http://www.teachercreated.com/books/3032**
>
> Click on Page 46, Site 1

The first task is to determine if a spider is an insect or an arachnid. Work with the students to find the answer by reading the information provided on the site. Have students complete the assignment and then tell them they may move on to the next task.

To keep track of which tasks the students have completed, have each student label a small construction paper fly with his/her name. Then the flies can move across the web as the students complete the tasks.

Upon completion of all the Web site activities, when they reach the center of the spider's web, consider giving students some form of recognition. This could be a certificate, a bookmark, a pencil, a sticker, or perhaps some trinket centered around the spider or tech-web theme.

Extension

Surf the Web to determine appropriate sites for more tasks. Look at these sites and determine what types of tasks you could have the students accomplish. You could also have the students make up their own tasks. They could design tasks based on Web sites and then switch them with other students to complete.

Name _____

The Spider's Web

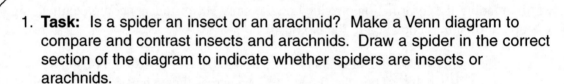

Directions: Use the information on the following Web sites to complete each task and move yourself to the center of the spider's web.

1. **Task:** Is a spider an insect or an arachnid? Make a Venn diagram to compare and contrast insects and arachnids. Draw a spider in the correct section of the diagram to indicate whether spiders are insects or arachnids.

   Go to **http://www.teachercreated.com/books/3032**

   Click on Page 46, Site 1

2. **Task:** Why does the spider have claws on its tarsus? Write a paragraph explaining the answer to this question. **Hint:** Move the icon over the fourth circular image to read about the legs of a spider.

   Go to **http://www.teachercreated.com/books/3032**

   Click on Page 46, Site 2

3. **Task:** How many materials are needed to make a spider glider? Write out a step-by-step plan for making the glider. Be sure to include what materials are needed and where you would get them.

   Go to **http://www.teachercreated.com/books/3032**

   Click on Page 46, Site 3

4. **Task:** Where do spiders go to learn new words? Answer this play-on-words. Then make up three more spider-related jokes for your friends.

   Go to **http://www.teachercreated.com/books/3032**

   Click on Page 46, Site 4

The Spider's Web *(cont.)*

5. **Task:** What are the two types of nets described in the book? Draw a picture of each.

> Go to **http://www.teachercreated.com/books/3032**

> Click on Page 47, Site 1

6. **Task:** In what temperatures do tarantulas live? In a paragraph, tell why tarantulas live in their chosen environments.

> Go to **http://www.teachercreated.com/books/3032**

> Click on Page 47, Site 2

7. **Task:** What colors are black widows? Draw and color a picture of the black widow and another spider that is a different color.

> Go to **http://www.teachercreated.com/books/3032**

> Click on Page 47, Site 3

8. **Task:** What can you use for eyes on a spider cake? Make up another dessert related to spiders, but this time, make it a dessert that the spiders would like to eat!

> Go to **http://www.teachercreated.com/books/3032**

> Click on Page 47, Site 4

9. **Task:** What is the main difference between a daddy longlegs and a regular spider? Make a graphic representation of the differences between these creatures. (You could make a Venn diagram, a compare/contrast chart, a picture diagram of the two subjects, etc.)

> Go to **http://www.teachercreated.com/books/3032**

> Click on Page 47, Site 5

Spider Outline for Bulletin Board

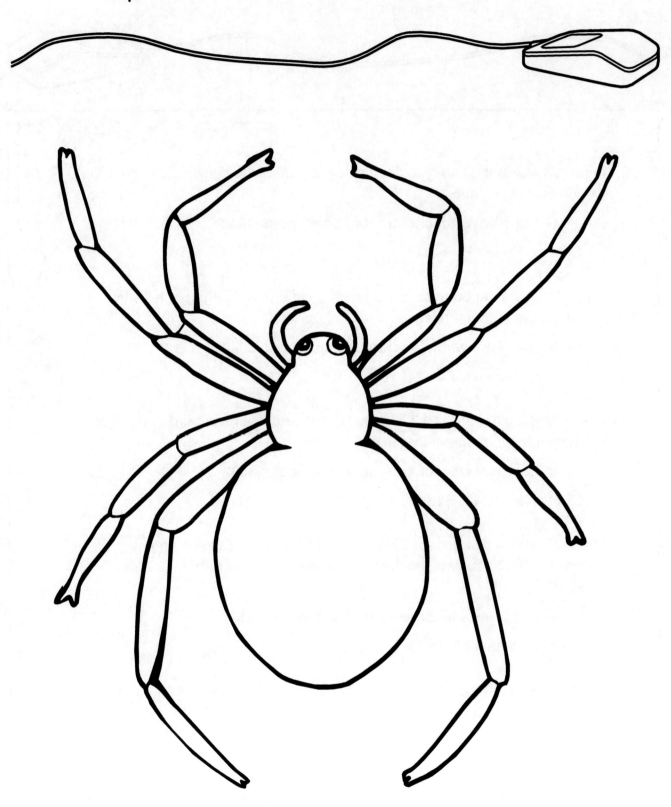

Book Outline for Bulletin Board

Fly Outlines for Bulletin Board

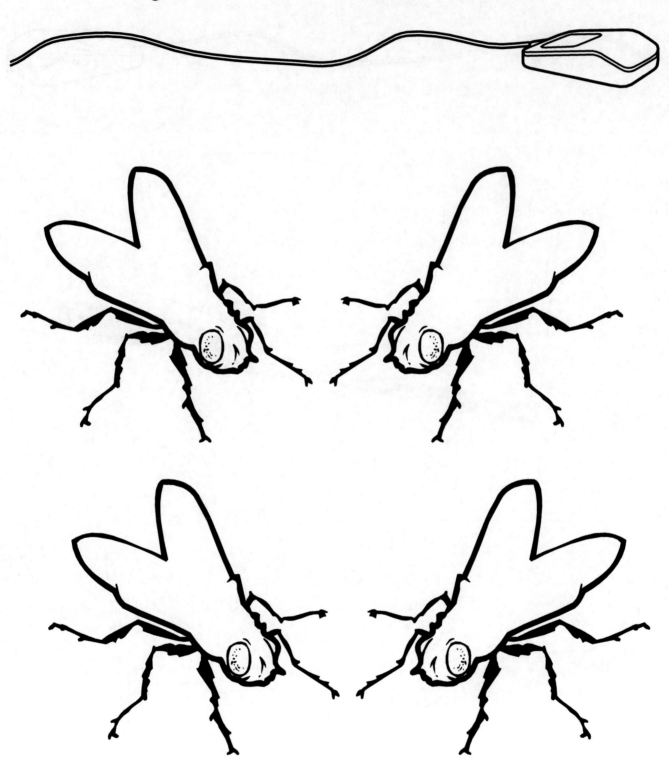

Video Conferencing

Objective

In this activity, students will

- use the video conference camera to conference with students from other schools in their district, state, country, and around the world.

Technology required

- Internet connection
- video conference camera
- *Cu-See Me* video conferencing software

Materials needed

- none

Description

This is a year-round project to promote good communication skills, research skills, geography skills, and understanding for other cultures. Once you have the equipment, you'll need to contact other schools who are also using the same video conferencing equipment. To find other schools, access the *Global Schoolhouse* site through the *Teacher Created Materials* Web site for this book:

Go to http://www.teachercreated.com/books/3032

Click on Page 51, Site 1

This gives you a list of schools around the world who are interested in video conferencing with other schools. Below are some things to keep in mind when choosing a school with which to partner:

- Check the time-zones of the two schools. Will the time difference be workable with your school schedule?
- Check the other school's calendar. Remember, summer in Australia is winter in the United States, and it will be more difficult to consistently meet with those students.
- Are the grade levels compatible? Many countries have this technology available at the secondary level, but not elementary. Make sure you understand the various terms that describe the different grade levels. It is different for every country.
- Do they speak English, or will there be a translator? If you teach a foreign language class, this would bring your problem to a minimum. However, most of us don't, so you'll want to make sure you speak the same language!
- Are the curriculums for the various schools compatible with your curriculum? If not, can adjustments be made?

Video Conferencing *(cont.)*

It may be best to have different groups of students video conference consistently with different schools. For example: have one group of 6–8 students meet with a school from Seattle, another group can conference with students from England, and yet another group can meet with students from Mexico. After the initial "getting to know each other" sessions, the students can begin to research broader topics, such as who has the longer migration, birds or whales?

Once you have selected your topics for the video conferences, the students from all schools begin to research the topics. They can then video conference with each school about once a week to share and compare information. Change the topics about every 4–6 weeks or as necessary to keep their interest. It is fun to compare cultural information, as well.

The *QuickCam* just sits on top of your computer and is frequently nicknamed "the eyeball" because of its appearance. It comes in black and white or color. It can also take still images or movies within your classroom. What a functional little camera!

Note: For more information on this exciting technology used for collaboration, see the book *Collaborative Projects Using the Internet* (published by Teacher Created Materials, 2001, **http://www.teachercreated.com**).

Extension

Have students design their own projects to complete with their collaborative buddies.

Addition

Objectives

In this activity, students will

- use a draw program to write addition equations.

Technology required

- *Kid Pix* or other graphics program
- printer

Materials needed

- any activity page of addition equations

Description

Use this lesson when learning or reviewing addition equations. Provide students with an activity page of addition number sentences. Demonstrate the use of the stamp tool to show appropriate numbers of objects to match the respective number sentences. Have the students complete the remainder of the addition equations on the sheet given to them. They must stamp objects for both addends and the sum.

After having students use the problems on the activity page, have them make up their own problems. This time, however, tell them not to stamp the answers to the problems. Instead, show the students how to print their work. Then, have the students exchange their student-created problems and try to solve them.

Extension

Follow similar procedures to demonstrate understanding of subtraction. Stamp appropriate objects to match equations and then partially erase or cross out stamps to show the difference.

Number Sense

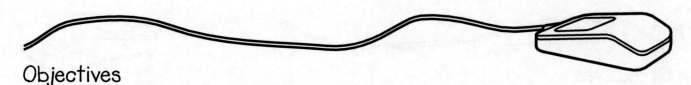

Objectives

In this activity, students will

- match the numerals 0–10 using stamps.
- print pictures with teacher assistance.

Technology required

- *Kid Pix* or other graphics program
- printer

Materials needed

- none

Description

Use this activity with students when they are just beginning to learn about numbers. Demonstrate how to stamp or draw the numerals on the screen. Once a numeral is on the page, demonstrate how to stamp the number of pictures to correspond with the numeral. Only four numerals will fit per page.

Students can then stamp or draw four numerals on each page, and then stamp the number of pictures to correspond with the numerals. Once this has been done for 0–10, allow students to print their pages.

Have the students also stamp their names on each page of numerals.

Extension

Have the students stamp the pictures in a domino pattern for each numeral. Students could also make playing cards for the numbers by stamping the correct number of hearts, diamonds, spades, or clubs.

Ordinal Numbers

Objective

In this activity, students will

- show their understanding of ordinal numbers.

Technology required

- *Kid Pix* or other graphics program
- printer

Materials needed

- none

Description

After introducing ordinal number words, have students use a draw program to type ordinal number words (first, second, third, etc.). (Teachers may want to consider preparing a template of these words for the students to save time.) Then using stamps, students make a row of ten stamps after each ordinal number word. Students can choose any stamps that they like for each row of ten.

To indicate their understanding of the ordinals, students use the draw tool to circle the appropriate stamp that matches the ordinal number word. For example, if the student typed the ordinal number word *sixth*, they would circle the sixth stamp in that row.

For students to practice different skills (or just to allow for individuality), you could allow them to perform different changes to each row. For example, in the first row, they have to circle the first stamp. In the second row, they make the second stamp larger than the rest. In the fifth row, they choose a different stamp for the fifth stamp or color it a different shade, etc. See the example on page 56. Once this is done, demonstrate how to print and allow your students to print their work.

Extension

Use number words along with the ordinal number words. Have students stamp the appropriate number of stamps to show understanding of the meaning of the number words. For example, the student types the number six and the ordinal number fourth. He/she would then make six stamps and circle the fourth stamp in the row.

Ordinal Numbers Example

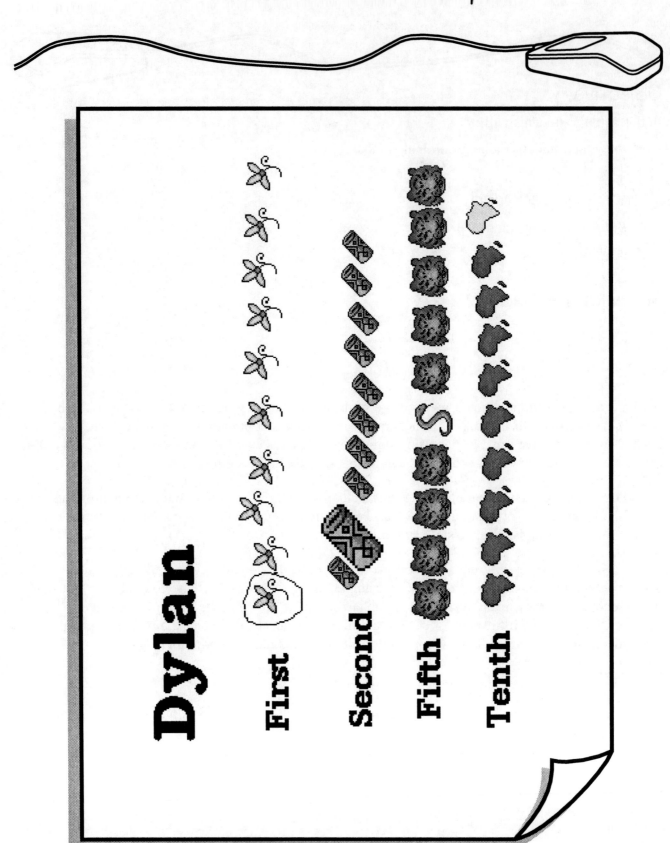

Patterns

Objectives

In this activity, students will

- stamp simple patterns using stamps.
- solve simple patterns.
- print pictures with teacher assistance.

Technology required

- *Kid Pix* or other graphics program
- printer

Materials needed

- none

Description

To begin this activity, demonstrate how to stamp a simple A-B pattern by stamping the letters **A B A B A B A B A B A** across the screen. Directly below the A-B pattern, demonstrate a pattern using alternating picture stamps.

Then, give students the opportunity to stamp simple patterns using the graphics program's stamps. After the students have practiced stamping patterns, have them get a clear screen. They now need to design a page border. The border can be up to three pictures in a pattern. Students should stamp the pattern around the edge of the paper (see example on page 58). The teacher can then decide what the students should put in the middle. Some suggestions for the middle are a hand-drawn picture, a computer-generated picture, a story, or the student's name. Once this is done, demonstrate how to print and allow your students to print their work.

Extension

Allow students to alter the size of the pattern by using the shift and options keys (in *Kid Pix*).

Patterns Example

Shapes

Objectives

In this activity, students will

- draw shapes using the tool bar.
- print out their assignments with teacher assistance.

Technology required

- *Kid Pix* or other graphics program
- printer

Materials needed

- none

Description

Demonstrate how to use the tool bar by showing the students how to use the rectangle, curve, and pencil. Then show them how to make a circle, oval, square, rectangle, and triangle.

Finally, give them the opportunity to practice using the different tools. After the students have had time to play with the application, have them clear their screens. Tell the students they have to draw a picture of a city (or whatever else the teacher assigns). They may only use circles, ovals, squares, rectangles, triangles, and lines. They may, however, use the eraser to change the shapes of objects. See the example on page 60. Once this is done, demonstrate how to print and allow the students to print their products.

Extension

The students can make other pictures using the different shapes (i.e., a house, a bear, a sun, a teepee, or a tree).

Shapes Example

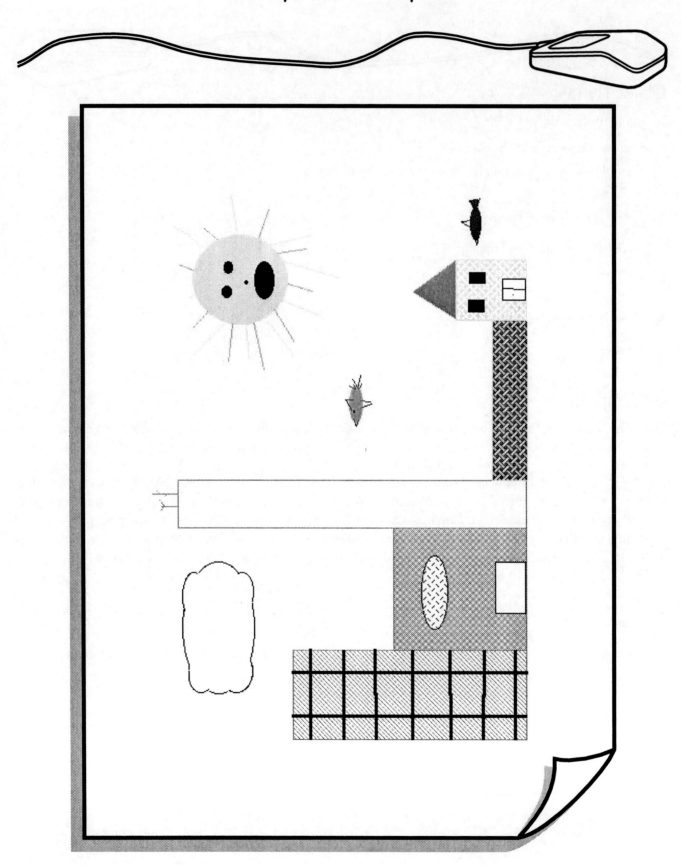

Computer Credit Card

Objectives

In this activity, students will

- design a computer credit card using a draw program.
- help teachers manage and monitor classroom use of the computers.

Technology required

- *Kid Pix* or other graphics program
- printer

Materials needed

- tagboard

Description

The students can help teachers manage computer use during the week. Have the students choose small graphics that represent themselves. They then need to each design a credit card-sized rectangle that has a stamp for the number of times each student should use the computer during the week.

Have each student start by drawing a rectangle in the graphics program. Inside the rectangle, they need to type or stamp the words, *Computer Credit Card.* See Step 1 on page 62. The second step is to add the stamps around the outside. The teacher needs to tell the students how many stamps to put on the card. See Step 2 on page 62. The final step is to use the moving truck to copy and paste the card on the page three more times. The students may have to retype the words in the middle of each card. See Step 3 on page 62. Have them then add their names to their cards and print their work.

Once the cards are printed on tagboard and cut apart, the teacher and the students can keep track of how many times each student has worked on a computer. After each visit, teachers can punch out one of the stamps on the card to show that some of the credit has been used. Teachers can collect the cards at the end of the week to see who has used the computers and how often the computers have been used.

The students should turn in the cards when they're all punched which means their computer time is finished for the week.

Extension

Have the students think of other reasons to design credit cards, such as library visits. Then have them make the cards, print them, and cut them apart.

Computer Credit Card Steps

Step 1

Step 2

Step 3

Design Your Dream Bedroom

Objectives

In this activity, students will

- use geometric concepts, properties, and relationships in problem-solving situations.
- communicate the reasoning used in solving these problems.

Technology required

- *AppleWorks*, *Microsoft Works*, or another drawing program
- *Microsoft Word, AppleWorks*, or other word processing program

Materials needed

- copies of *Bedroom Floorplan* (page 64) for the students
- copies of *Furniture Choices* (page 65) for the students

Description

Tell the students the following scenario. Record the important facts on the board as you tell them.

- You and your family are moving to a new house. Included is the floor plan for your bedroom (page 64). Your parents have agreed to allow you to choose and arrange your own bedroom furniture as long as you meet these criteria:

    1. You must include a sleeping area, a work area, a play area, and appropriate walk space.

    2. You must select from the parent-approved furniture provided (page 65).

- Using a drawing program, draw the floor plan of your own bedroom, including furniture placement (one $^1/_4$" square = 1 square foot).

- Then, using a word processing program, write a description of your new bedroom. In your description, include which furniture you chose and why; where you put the furniture and why; and evidence that you met the criteria set by your parents.

Extension

The students could plan the layout of their entire homes, classrooms, school, etc.

Name _____

Bedroom Floorplan

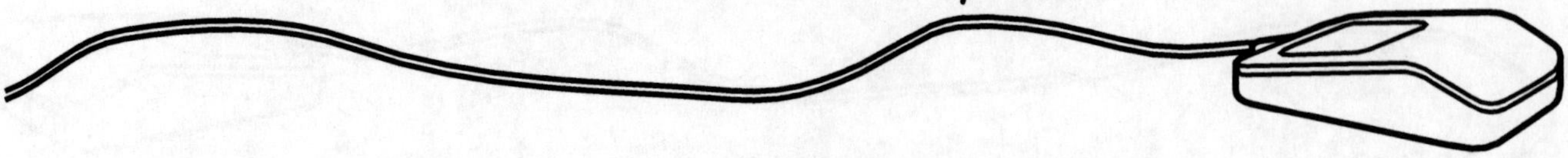

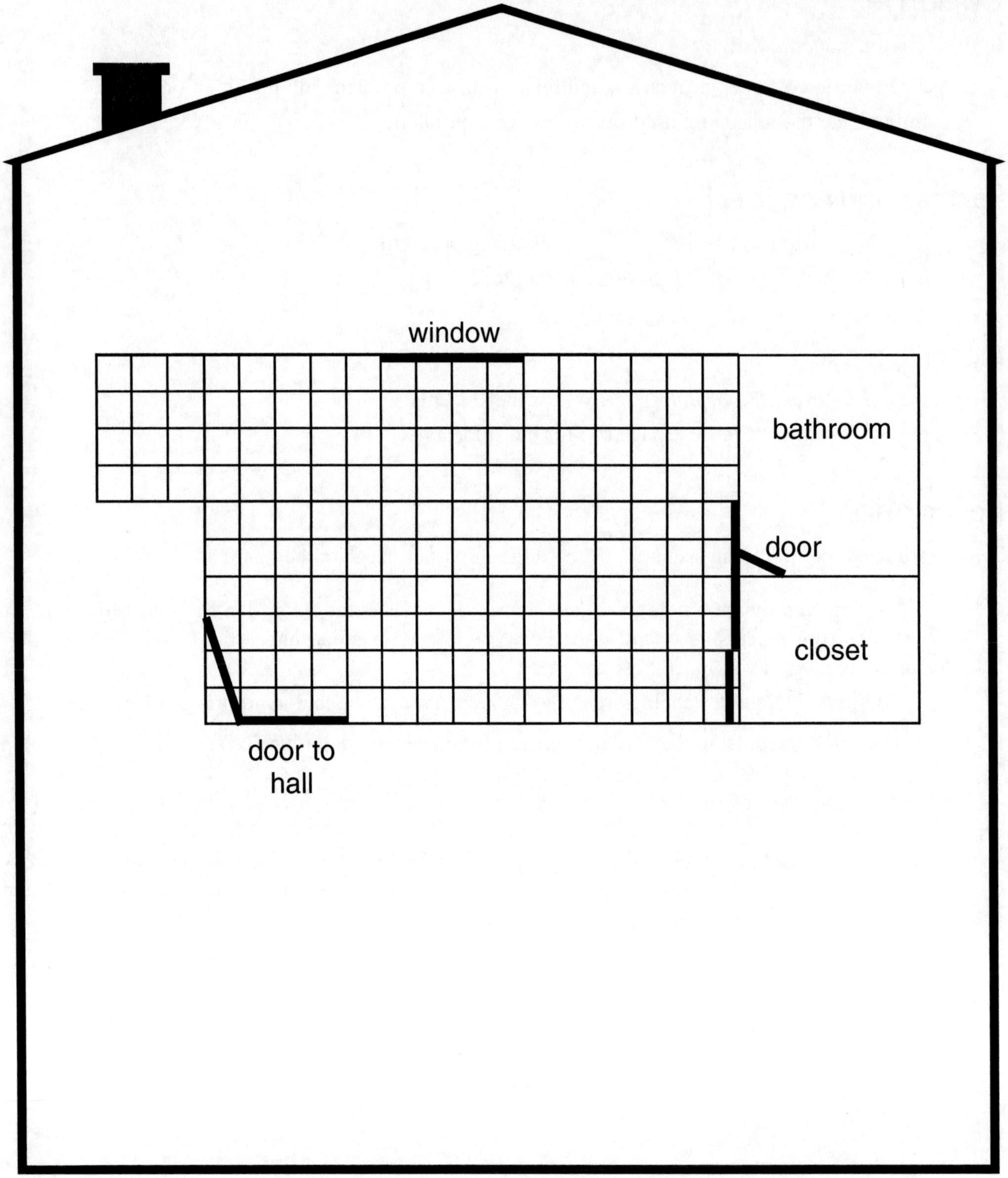

window

bathroom

door

closet

door to
hall

Furniture Choices

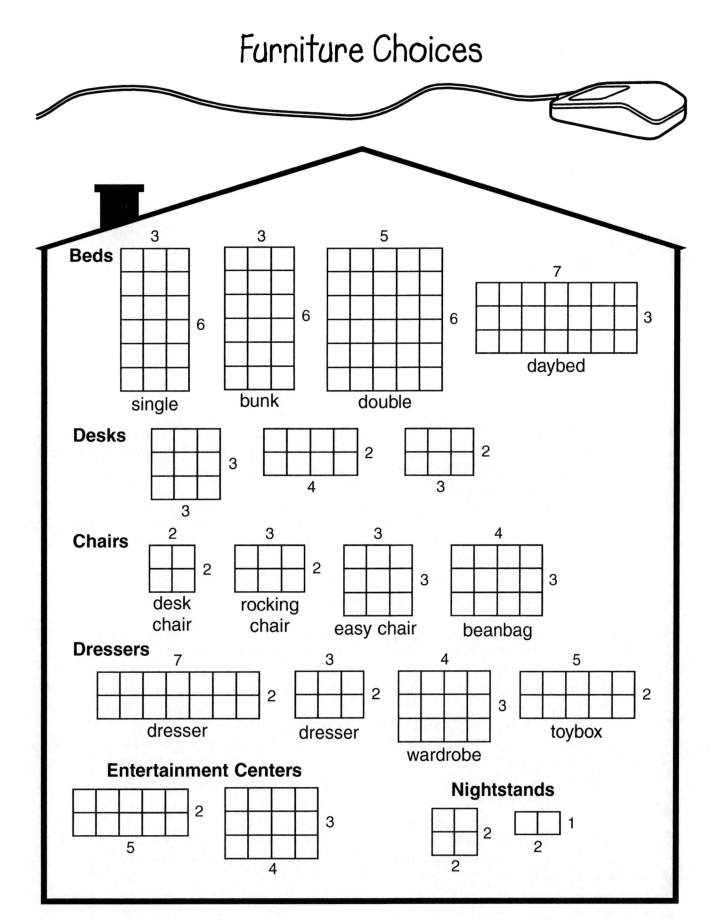

Beds

3 — 6 — single
3 — 6 — bunk
5 — 6 — double
7 — 3 — daybed

Desks

3 — 3
2 — 4
2 — 3

Chairs

2 — 2 — desk chair
3 — 2 — rocking chair
3 — 3 — easy chair
4 — 3 — beanbag

Dressers

7 — 2 — dresser
3 — 2 — dresser
4 — 3 — wardrobe
5 — 2 — toybox

Entertainment Centers

2 — 5
3 — 4

Nightstands

2 — 2
1 — 2

Fitness Challenge

Objective

In this activity, students will

- document and evaluate their own physical fitness.

Technology required

- spreadsheet program
- printer

Materials needed

- quarter sheets of paper on which the students will enter their fitness challenge statistics

Description

Most schools have certain grades that participate in fitness testing each year. As the students complete each activity, have them record their abilities on small sheets of paper in each of the following areas: one mile run, sit-ups, pull-ups/push-ups, and other activities specific to the school.

Before testing begins, have each student create a spreadsheet with a column for each fitness test that will be given to the students. Tell the students to enter the names of nine of their classmates in the first column. Teachers might want to consider assigning each student an identification number. Then, when the data is recorded and entered, the students who did not do well on the test will not be embarrassed. The students will fill in the scores after the testing is complete. As the students complete each test, collect all the slips of paper so that students do not misplace them.

Once all the fitness tests are done, have the students enter their own scores and those of their nine classmates. Show the students how to find the averages of the scores using the spreadsheet formulas. As a class, determine the best boy's and best girl's scores for the different tests. Once this is done, they should create a bar graph showing the best boy's, best girl's, and average scores.

They can then create an individual graph with their own scores, the best boy's/girl's scores, and the average scores. Print copies of these individual graphs and send them home with an explanation of the tests the students completed.

Extension

Have the students complete graphs for the entire class. They can find the mean, median, mode, and range of each set of scores. A number of graphs could be designed to share the class' fitness information with others.

Flashcards on the Net

Objective

In this activity, students will

- practice addition, subtraction, multiplication, and division facts using the computer and the Internet.

Technology required

- Internet connection

Materials needed

- none

Description

As a fun way to practice math basics, the students can use a great Web site called *Education 4 Kids*. The site itself is pretty self-explanatory, so once the students are connected, the teacher just needs to monitor their work.

Students begin by accessing the *Education 4 Kids* Web site through the *Teacher Created Materials* Web site for this book:

>   Go to **http://www.teachercreated.com/books/3032**

>   Click on Page 67, Site 1

Once the Web site is loaded, the students can choose the type of math activity, complexity of the problems, and the range of numbers that will be used. They can also turn on the score, choose to be timed, and choose how to view the problems.

Students read the problems and type the correct answers. The computer keeps track of the number they get right and gives the student that information at the end of the session.

Extension

The students may increase the level of difficulty or the numbers used in the problems. Have the students design their own math problems for the computer. See if they can use a program to make them interactive.

Geometric Greats

Objectives

In this activity, students will

- use a drawing program to create different types of geometric angles and triangles.
- practice finding the radius and diameter of a circle.

Technology required

- *AppleWorks*, *Microsoft Works*, or another drawing program
- printer

Materials needed

- plastic protractors (clear is best—never use metal protractors on a computer screen)

Description

Geometric Greats is actually broken down into three separate assignments. Use this activity during the study of angles and triangles in a geometry unit.

The first assignment is drawing the different types of angles: acute, obtuse, and right angles. Give the students a list of angle measurements such as: 90°, 38°, 115°, 145°, 180°, and 67°. Using a protractor, the students draw the angles, label the measurements, and label if they are acute, obtuse, or right angles. When they complete this assignment, they should print it, re-measure their angles, and move to assignment two.

The second assignment is creating the different types of triangles. The students must use the following measurements to create a scalene, isosceles, and equilateral triangle: 1.75 inches, 1.5 inches, 1.25 inches, and 1 inch. Since many drawing programs have inch grids on the screen, the numbers here were given in inches. So if teachers want to use metric measurements instead of standard, they should use round measurements for centimeters (i.e., 7 cm, 6 cm, and 5 cm) and have the students use rulers to judge the triangles' sides. They need to use these numbers in any combination to create the triangles listed. After drawing the triangles, they should label the triangles and print their work. After printing their work, they should check the triangle side measurements for accuracy.

Geometric Greats *(cont.)*

The last assignment relates to finding the radii and diameters of circles. The students can hold down the shift key while they draw their circles to give them perfect circles.

Have them draw five different circles with the following radii or diameters:

    Circle 1: radius of 2 inches

    Circle 2: diameter of 6 inches

    Circle 3: diameter of 8.5 inches

    Circle 4: radius of 3.5 inches

    Circle 5: radius of 4.5 inches

The measurements here were given in inches because many drawing programs have inch grids on the screen. So if teachers want to use metric measurements instead of standard, they should use round measurements for centimeters (i.e., 3 cm, 15 cm, 20 cm, 8 cm, and 11 cm) and have the students use rulers to judge the diameters and radii of the circles.

When they have drawn all five circles, they should print their work and check it for accuracy.

Extension

Have the students decide upon measurements for their classmates to draw. Students could even design pictures that combine figures of exact measurements. For example, draw a picture that has three circles of 3, 5, and 6 inch radii; two scalene triangles; four acute angles; etc.

Geometric Greats Example

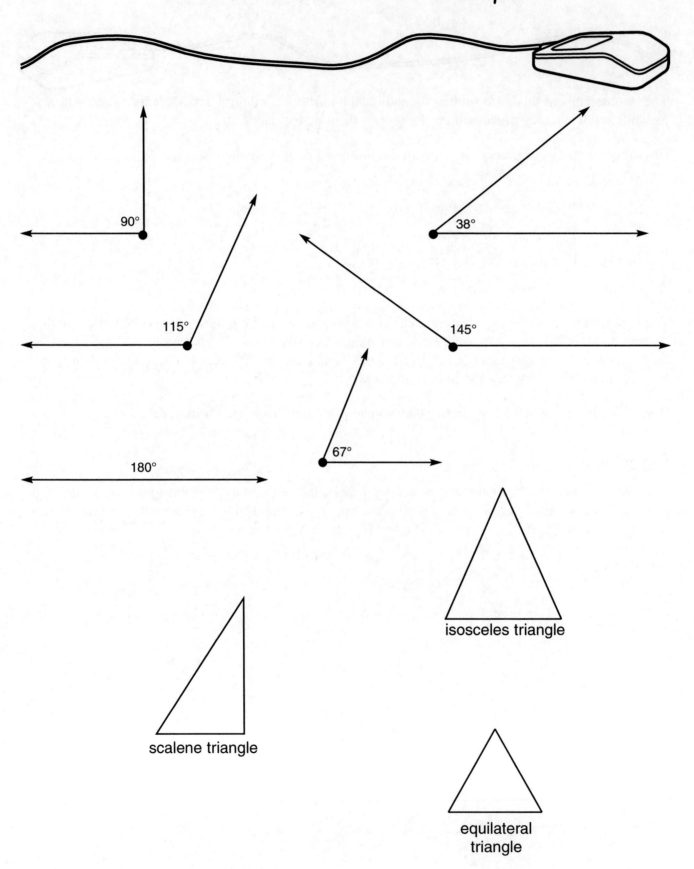

Tessellations!

Objectives

In this activity, students will

- be exposed to the life and work of M.C. Escher.
- define the term *tessellation*.
- review geometric terms (shape, square, triangle, hexagon, rectangle, etc.).
- demonstrate knowledge and understanding of the slide and rotation transformation.

Technology required

- *AppleWorks*, *Microsoft Works*, or another drawing program
- *TesselMania!* software (optional)
- printer

Materials needed

- 3" x 3" square pieces of tagboard
- 9" x 12" construction paper
- pencils and markers

Description

Introduce the students to the artwork of M.C. Escher by viewing his prints that include tessellations (especially his metamorphosis series). Define *tessellation* as a puzzle made up of repeated use of a shape to completely fill up a plane with no gaps or overlapping. Ask the kids to think of examples of tessellations in our everyday life (tiles on floor, bricks on patio, patterns on wrapping paper, fabric, etc.).

Using a square as an example, demonstrate the two basic techniques for transformation—slide and rotation. See the diagrams on page 72. You may want to use an overhead projector for this.

If possible, introduce the *TesselMania!* program. The program is very user-friendly and when printed (in black and white or color), the tessellations are worth framing!

If the school does not have *TesselMania!*, have the students tessellate figures by copying and pasting them to cover a page. See the examples on page 73.

Extension

On the computer, the students can progress to more difficult shapes and transformation techniques in the *TesselMania!* program. Students can also make tessellations with pattern blocks or attribute blocks.

Transformations–Slides and Rotations

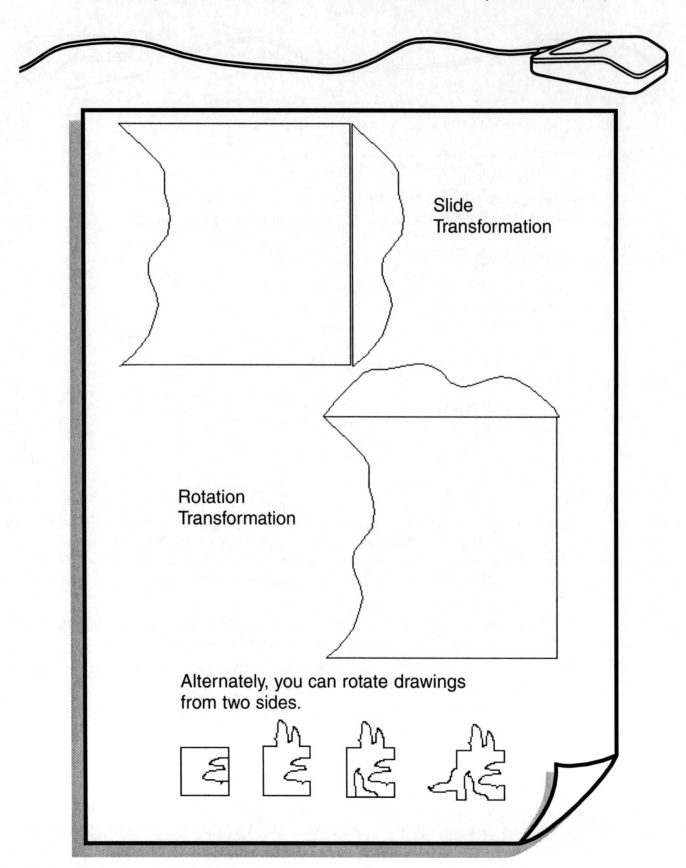

Slide
Transformation

Rotation
Transformation

Alternately, you can rotate drawings
from two sides.

Tessellations! Examples

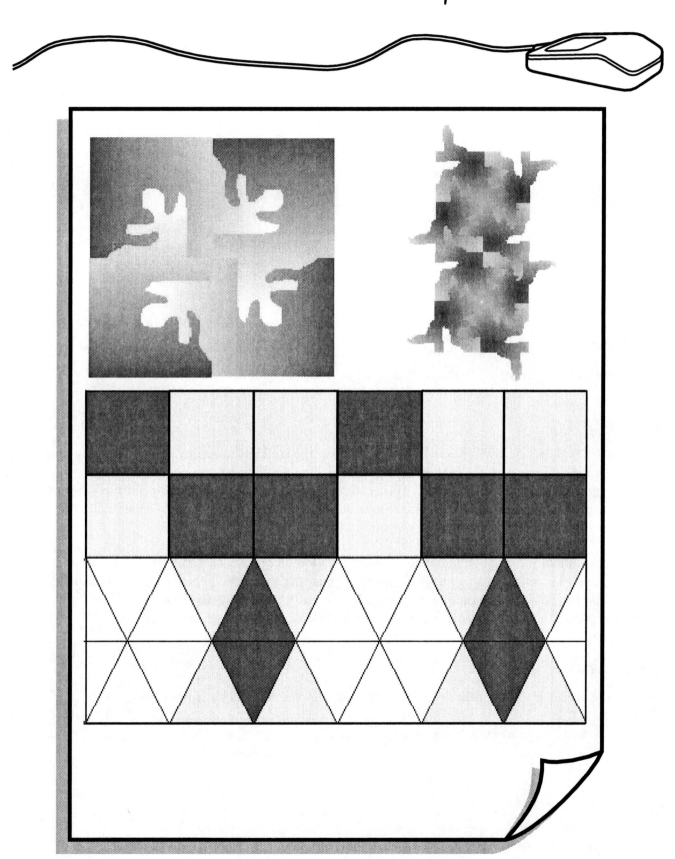

Acorn Pond

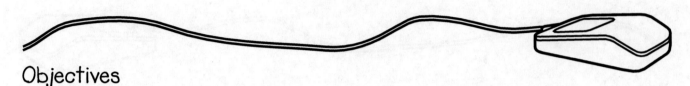

Objectives

In this activity, students will

- research animals in a particular season.
- share information with the class.
- display information on a bulletin board in the classroom.

Technology required

- *Sammy's Science House*
- printer

Materials needed

- bulletin board materials to make an Acorn Pond

Description

Explore the *Sammy's Science House* CD-ROM. Direct the students to Acorn Pond. They can choose a season by clicking icons on the bottom of the screen. Double-clicking on an animal will give the students information about that animal. Have them each choose one animal and print the information. Have each student read, or have someone read to the student, information about the animal. The student can then prepare a report about the animal for the class.

Display the animal information in the appropriate location on an "Acorn Pond" bulletin board. Divide a pond into the four seasons using yarn or markers. Then, the students can make figures of their animals to be put on the board. For example, in the winter Acorn Pond display, the snake would be in the rocks for hibernation. In spring, the snake may be on the rocks soaking up the sun.

Extension

Use other sources to supplement research. Students can sort animals by habitat, food, body characteristics, etc. Develop a multimedia project by making a scene of Acorn Pond and having the students record information by video or audio means.

Bugs!

Objective

In this activity, students will

- show their understanding of the parts of an insect.

Technology required

- *Kid Pix* or other graphics program

Materials needed

- none

Description

Teachers can use this activity as practice or an assessment of a unit on bugs.

The students will create an insect using the draw tool in a graphics program such as *Kid Pix*. Make sure the students include and correctly label the different parts of an insect in their drawings: three body parts, antennae, and six legs.

Have the students draw their bugs in the appropriate habitats.

Extension

Students can draw a number of different kinds of insects that might inhabit the same environment.

Habitats for Mammals

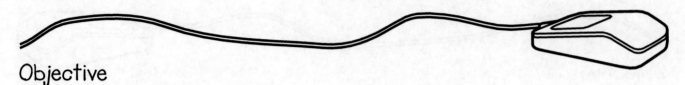

Objective

In this activity, students will

- show their understanding of appropriate animal habitats for mammals.

Technology required

- *Kid Pix* or other graphics program
- Internet connection

Materials needed

- none

Description

Teachers can complete this lesson after a unit on mammals and their habitats. Have the students use a graphics program to draw and color habitats for mammals. Once the students have drawn their habitats, have them go on the Internet to find pictures of their animals to copy into the habitats they designed. For example, a student might draw a picture of tall, snow-capped mountains. For that habitat, he or she could copy pictures of mountain sheep or grizzly bears to place in the picture.

After the students have completed their individual pictures, combine multiple pictures into a slide show.

Extension

Students could create individual slide shows that illustrate many different environments and the animals that inhabit them.

Making Plants

Objective

In this activity, students will

- draw and label the parts of a plant using a computer drawing program.

Technology required

- *Kid Pix* or other graphics program

Materials needed

- plant pictures
- plant part names

Description

Using a graphics program, have the students draw pictures of plants. They can use the paint bucket to color the plants.

Once this is done, have the students use the text tool to type the plant part names. See page 78 for an example. Teachers might want to have these part names written on the board for student reference.

After the students have completed their individual pictures, help them combine the pictures into a plant slide show.

Extension

The students could make individual slide shows. The initial slides/cards/scenes could show each individual part of the plant closely. The following slides/cards/scenes could combine parts of plants to make a complete example.

Making Plants Example

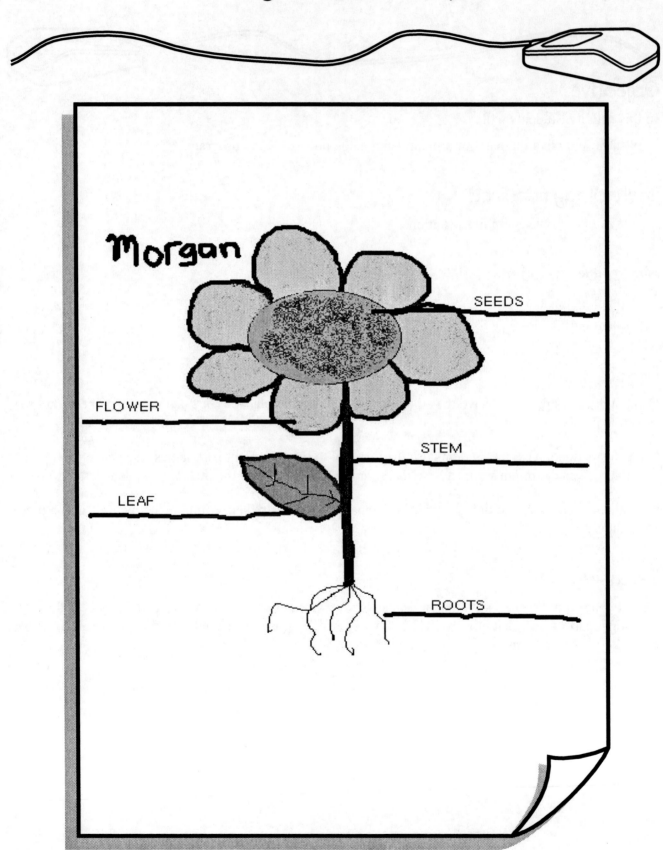

Mr. Bones

Objective

In this activity, students will

- build the human skeleton using knowledge gained on an Internet site.

Technology required

- Internet connection

Materials needed

- none

Description

Students begin by accessing the *Virtual Body* Web site through the *Teacher Created Materials* Web site for this book:

> Go to **http://www.teachercreated.com/books/3032**

> Click on Page 79, Site 1

You may need to download a free plug-in to run the programs at this site. Turn up the volume on your computer and enjoy the **Bones Narrated** link on this fantastic Web site. After listening to the narrated tour, have the students try their hands at putting skeletons together correctly using the **Build a Skeleton** link. **Zoom in!** is a neat link as well. It will show the students an up-close look at the major bones.

Extension

Students can also learn about the heart, brain, and digestive tract from this Web site.

Postcards from Space

Objectives

In this activity, students will

- demonstrate knowledge of characteristics of planets gathered from nonfiction reading by writing and drawing about them.
- demonstrate understanding of how to address a postcard appropriately.

Technology required

- *Microsoft Word, AppleWorks*, or other word processing program
- *AppleWorks, Microsoft Works*, or other drawing program
- printer

Materials needed

- nonfiction resources for research (electronic or text)
- tagboard and glue

Description

Have each student choose a planet to research. Using resources provided by you, students will research their planets. This can be combined with shared reading lessons about the planets during which the students accumulate more data.

During computer time, have them write a letter containing factual information about their planets using a word processing program. This letter should be written as if the students were visiting the planet and writing about what they see. Teachers of kindergarten or early first grade might consider doing the written part of this activity as a whole-class lesson.

At a follow-up computer time, have the students draw pictures that illustrate knowledge about their planets. For example, if the student chose the planet Saturn, he/she might include the rings, make appropriate color choices, or place it next to another planet to compare size. Have the students label their drawings to show what they have learned.

Once both computer assignments are complete, have the students print them separately. Then, students can glue their letters to the reverse sides of their pictures. They now have large postcards to send to a parent or loved one. See the sample provided on page 81.

Extension

Have the students make a slide show with pictures about their planets.

Postcards from Space Example

Dear Mom,

I'm on a planet that is all red. The earth looks very close compared to other planets. I am very thirsty and want some water.

Love,

Laura

To: Mom

1234 West Anytown Drive

Hometown, CA 55555

Back of card

Front of card

Seasons of the Year

Objective

In this activity, students will

- show their understanding of the seasons of the year.

Technology required

- *Kid Pix* or other graphics program
- printer

Materials needed

- none

Description

Teachers should use this activity at the conclusion of a unit on the seasons of the year. The students begin by drawing a picture of one of the four seasons. They need to include lots of details in their pictures.

Next, have the students write stories for their pictures using the text component of their draw program or a word processor. The stories can be in the form of narratives, poems, or descriptions.

Finally, print the pictures and text and let the students color their masterpieces.

Extension

Have the students write a longer story that includes details about all four seasons. Then, students would have to draw at least four pictures for their stories (one for each season).

82

Weather and Butterflies

Objective

In this activity, students will

- demonstrate knowledge of weather and butterflies.

Technology required

- *Kid Pix* or other graphics program

Materials needed

- science reference materials (electronic and/or print)
- 3" x 5" cards

Description

Have each student choose a subject to research, either weather or butterflies. As they read the reference materials, the students must find three to five facts about the topic. They need to write each fact on a 3" x 5" card. Have the students self and peer edit their cards.

The students then open *Kid Pix* or some other graphics program. Have the students type each fact and design a picture to go with it. So, each student will make two pictures. After the facts and pictures are finished, the students need to verbally record their facts onto the slides.

Work with the students to put together all the slides into a class slide show. The students can choose how their own slides will transition from one to another.

Extension

Allow students the opportunity to produce their own slide show with many more details about their topics.

Contour Map Makers

Objectives

In this activity, students will

- make their own contour maps using a drawing program.
- draw one map to show elevation and one map to show depth.

Technology required

- *AppleWorks*, *Microsoft Works*, or another drawing program
- printer

Materials needed

- none

Description

Teachers should use this assignment after introducing the students to contour maps. Before moving to the computers, the students need to practice making these maps on paper. Then, they can go into the drawing program and use the various draw tools to create one contour map to show elevation and one to show depth.

The students' maps must start at sea level. The maps need to be labeled on each level. The students must use a variation of color to demonstrate the elevation and depth. If possible, each student should print one copy in color, and teachers can display them on a bulletin board.

Extension

Students can extend this assignment by creating a variety of maps using a draw or paint program. They can also search for contour maps on the Internet, through NASA or oceanography sites.

Contour Map Makers Example

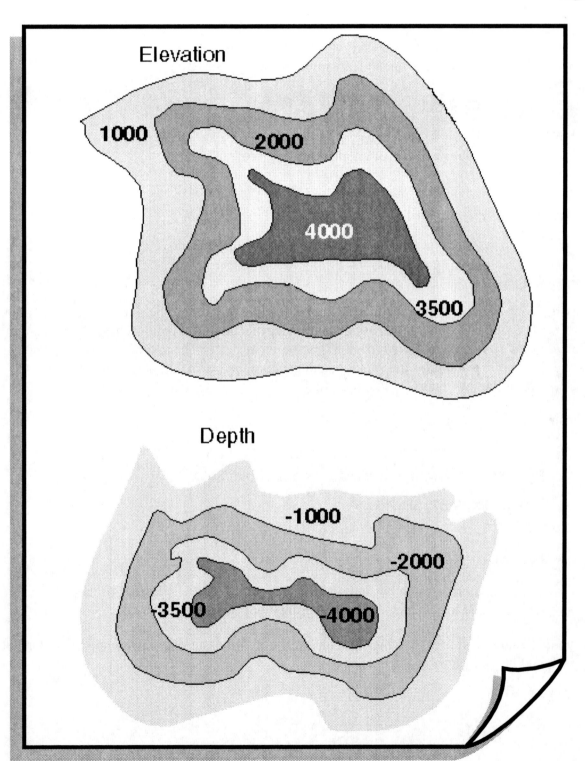

Elevation

Depth

Dinosaur Research

Objective

In this activity, students will

- investigate a dinosaur time line to learn about these amazing creatures.

Technology required

- Internet connection
- *AppleWorks, Microsoft Works*, or another drawing program
- printer

Materials needed

- copies of *Dinosaur Time Line Research* (page 87) for the students

Description

This assignment combines using the Internet and a drawing program to help the students learn about dinosaurs. The students work on this assignment independently or in pairs. They follow the directions on the *Dinosaur Time Line Research* (page 87) assignment sheet. The assignment incorporates higher-level thinking skills, reading for information, and creating their own animals to include the characteristics of the two dinosaurs that they studied.

Demonstrate how to access the *Dinosaur Time Line Gallery* Web site through the Teacher Created Materials Web site for this book:

> Go to **http://www.teachercreated.com/books/3032**
>
> Click on Page 87, Site 1

Extension

Students can extend their research by studying more about the geologic history of their area, interviewing workers at local parks, and volunteering a day at visitor centers.

Have your students send their drawings into the Web site's dinosaur drawing competition. One of the students could be the winner of the big prize!

Name _____

Dinosaur Time Line Research

Access the *Dinosaur Time Line Gallery* Web site:

     Go to **http://www.teachercreated.com/books/3032**

     Click on Page 87, Site 1

Click on the *Dinosaur Time Line Gallery* link and answer the following questions.

1. How many different time periods are represented? _____

   _____

2. Which of these time periods have you heard of before today? _____

   _____

Click on a link for one of the last four time periods in the time line.

3. Name the dinosaurs during this time period. _____

   _____

4. Pick your two favorite dinosaurs after browsing through the various animals. Which two did you pick? _____

   _____

5. List the physical qualities of each animal you chose (height, weight, etc.): _____

   _____

6. Which of the two animals was taller? _____

7. Which of the two animals was heavier? _____

8. What other characteristics can you use to compare and contrast the two animals?

   _____

9. If you had to go back in time and become one of these two animals, which one would you like to be and why? _____

   _____

   _____

Go into a drawing program and draw a new dinosaur that is a combination of the two dinosaurs you compared above. Give the new dinosaur a new name and explain (logically) why you gave it that name. Include a description of the size of the new animal and other important information that people should know about your unique animal.

Earth Viewer

Objectives

In this activity, students will

- use a Web site to connect with a satellite and view Earth at any moment.
- use their knowledge of latitude and longitude to view different positions of Earth.

Technology required

- *Microsoft Word, AppleWorks,* or other word processing program
- Internet connection

Materials needed

- copies of *Earth Viewer Welcomes You* (pages 89–90) for the students

Description

The students can work on this activity independently or with a partner. Begin by giving an introductory lesson showing the Web site and the variety of activities one can do with it.

Demonstrate for students how to access the *Earth and Moon Viewer* Web site through the *Teacher Created Materials* Web site for this book:

> Go to **http://www.teachercreated.com/books/3032**
>
> Click on Page 89, Site 1

Once the Web site opens, show the students where to click in order to complete *Earth Viewer Welcomes You* activity page (pages 89–90).

It is important to note that this lesson is set up for January. The questions may not coordinate with views from other months. However, the teacher may want to have the students view this once a month or every other month so they can literally see the rotation of the earth. Make sure the altitude, latitude, and longitude positions stay the same to create an accurate comparison of the different months.

When the students work on this, they should either answer the questions in a word processing program or simply write the answers on paper.

Extension

Have the students use the Web site to view the region where they live.

Students can extend their research to looking at Moon Viewer using the same Web site. They can look at the various longitudes, latitudes, and altitudes of the lunar satellite.

Name _____

Earth Viewer Welcomes You

Access the *Earth and Moon Viewer* Web site:

>   Go to **http://www.teachercreated.com/books/3032**
>   Click on Page 89, Site 1

Click on the highlighted words *latitude, longitude,* and *altitude* under **Viewing the Earth**.

This link will take you to a **View Above Earth** window that gives you the current view of the earth's surface.

Type in these numbers for latitude, longitude, and altitude. (Do not use commas to indicate place value.)

- latitude: 47 North

- longitude: 7 East

- altitude: 35785 kilometers above Earth's surface

Click on the **View Earth** button, and answer the following questions:

>   1. From this view, what entire continent can you see?
>
>   _____
>
>   2. What continents can you only see parts of?
>
>   _____
>
>   _____
>
>   3. Name three oceans found in this view.
>
>   _____
>
>   _____
>
>   4. How are night and day indicated? _____
>
>   _____

Click the **Back** button on your browser menu.

(over)

Earth Viewer Welcomes You (cont.)

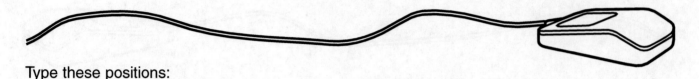

Type these positions:

- latitude: 40 North
- longitude: 120 West
- altitude: 35785 kilometers above Earth's surface

Click on the **View Earth** button, and answer the following questions:

5. What part of the world is showing now?

   _____

6. Where is the sun in relation to this side of the globe?

   _____

7. What three oceans do you see here?

   _____

   _____

Under the picture, change the altitude reading to 100 km and click the **Update** button.

8. What happened to your view?

   _____

   _____

Change the readings under the picture to explore the following positions. Be sure you push the **Update** button after changing the readings.

latitude:	30 South	latitude:	0 South	latitude:	165 North
longitude:	135 East	longitude:	0 West	longitude:	180 West
altitude:	335000 km	altitude:	35000 km	altitude:	5000 km

9. Write at least three paragraphs describing the differences in each position. Make sure you write specific information. Also, draw a picture of each position to go with your paragraphs.

Electrical Circuits

Objective

In this activity, students will

- draw a complete circuit.

Technology required

- *Kid Pix* or other graphics program
- printer

Materials needed

- none

Description

Prior to the lesson, the students should have hands-on experience with batteries, bulbs, wires, battery holders, and sockets. After exploring various ways to make a bulb light, the students will be asked to draw a complete circuit using a graphics program such as *Kid Pix*. Once the drawings are complete, have the students print them.

Each student's drawing must include:

- one bulb
- one socket
- three wires
- two batteries
- two battery holders

Teachers can assess the drawings to see if the students have shown exactly where the wires must attach to the light bulbs. Also, do the students have both batteries arranged correctly according to the plus/minus charges?

Extension

The teacher can design mystery boxes to challenge the students. Each box will have a variety of circuits inside with brads on the outside connected to wires. The students will draw what they think is inside each box. They can use one bulb, one battery, and two wires to make their predictions.

Endangered Animals in Their Habitats

Objectives

In this activity, students will

- conduct research about endangered animals.
- determine their habitats.
- provide specific information about their animals.

Technology required

- *PowerPoint, HyperStudio, Scene Slate,* or another multimedia program

Materials needed

- research materials on endangered animals and their habitats
- pictures of the animals in their habitats
- copies of *Multimedia/Slide Show Planning Sheet* (page 43) for the groups

Description

Working in groups of three or four, each group chooses an animal to research and determines the habitat type or region in which it lives. Groups conduct the research over a period of weeks to include specific information requested by the teacher. Assign all groups the task of finding similar types of information, such as body covering, dietary habits, cause for endangered status, etc.

Once the students have completed their research, they can begin planning their multimedia projects. Groups begin by planning their slides/scenes/cards as they will appear in their multimedia project. This planning should be done away from the computer using the *Multimedia/Slide Show Planning Sheet* (page 43).

Once the teacher has approved the planning sheet for the group, each group needs computer time to create the actual slides/scenes/cards that show their animal and the information that they have found during the course of their research. They may have a menu with links to other slides/scenes/cards that contain the different categories of information.

All projects must include scanned or other digital images, sound, and text. The students should present their projects to the class.

Extension

All the projects could be linked together to a main card or scene that contains the habitats or regions to which the animals belong. The user clicks on the habitat or region and another menu displaying the endangered animals that reside there is presented. The user then clicks on the animal that they would like to learn more about.

Meet the Corals

Objectives

In this activity, students will

- learn about various types of coral in our oceans.
- create their own coral garden by hand or using a drawing program.

Technology required

- *AppleWorks*, *Microsoft Works*, or other drawing program
- Internet connection

Materials needed

- drawing materials (optional)
- copies of *Meet the Corals Online* (pages 94–95) for the students

Description

This assignment allows the students to go on a virtual field trip to different coral gardens that exist in our oceans. When they travel, they first go to *Fisheye View Cam* to see the different corals.

Show the students how to access the *Fisheye View Cam* Web site through the *Teacher Created Materials* Web site for this book:

> **Go to http://www.teachercreated.com/books/3032**
>
> Click on Page 94, Site 1

Students can then travel to *Sea World's Coral and Coral Reefs* Web site for more research.

> Go to **http://www.teachercreated.com/books/3032**
>
> Click on Page 95, Site 1

The students work on this assignment independently and must read and answer the questions on the *Meet the Corals Online* assignment sheet (pages 94–95). When this is completed, they draw their own coral garden either in a drawing program or on paper.

Extension

Students can extend their research to learn how pollution is endangering many coral gardens around the world.

Name _____

Meet the Corals Online

Access the *Fisheye View Cam* Web site:

> Go to **http://www.teachercreated.com/books/3032**
>
> Click on Page 94, Site 1

Scroll down the screen and click on **Meet the Corals**.

Click on the first thumbnail picture under **Recent Views of the Fisheye View Cam**. Look at the detail of this picture entitled *Coral Reef Scene*. There are several different types of coral in this picture.

Click on **Next Image** to find a close-up image of the different types of coral.

Continue to click on the different images until you return to the *Coral Reef Scene*.

Answer the questions below. You are welcome to view the images again to help you answer the questions.

1. Tell four differences between green brain coral, bubble coral, and plate coral.

   • _____

   • _____

   • _____

   • _____

2. Notice the titles of the pictures. They give the names for the different types of coral. Why do you think each type of coral received the name it did?

   a. plate coral— _____

   b. pink leather coral— _____

   c. fox coral— _____

   d. purple mushroom coral— _____

3. What is the difference between green brain coral, open brain coral, and pink brain coral?

   _____

   _____

Meet the Corals Online *(cont.)*

After you have viewed the *Fisheye View Cam* images, you may go to *Sea World's Coral and Coral Reefs* Web site to answer the following questions.

Begin by accessing *Sea World's Coral and Coral Reefs* Web site:

> Go to **http://www.teachercreated.com/books/3032**

> Click on Page 95, Site 1

Click on the link for **Physical Characteristics**.

4. Is coral a plant or an animal? _____

5. What is a group of coral called? _____

6. What is the largest type of coral called? The smallest? _____

_____

Click the **Back** button on your browser menu.

Click on the link for **Coral Reefs** to answer the next questions.

7. How are hard corals created?_____

_____

8. Name and describe the three different types of coral reefs. You may draw pictures to help you explain your information. However, you must also have at least three sentences to go with each picture.

_____

_____

_____

9. Name four kinds of coral you would put in your own coral garden.

_____   _____

_____   _____

   a. Draw a detailed, color picture of what your coral garden would look like. You may create your picture by hand or in a draw program.

   b. Label the different types of coral you have and any other plants or animals you would like to have in your garden.

Oceanography Multimedia Projects

Objectives

In this activity, students will

- create a comprehensive multimedia project.
- conduct research including information about two student-selected animals and plants that thrive in the ocean.

Technology required

- *PowerPoint, HyperStudio, Scene Slate,* or another multimedia program
- Internet connection
- digital camera

Materials needed

- research materials
- copies of the *Teacher Assessment* sheets (pages 98–99) for teacher evaluation of the presentations
- copies of the *Student Assessment sheets* (pages 100–101) for the students
- copies of *Multimedia/Slide Show Planning Sheet* (page 43) for the groups

Description

This is a long-term project incorporating many language skills as well as science and technology skills. Each student group of two students must pick research questions that cover a specific topic related to oceanography. Then the students decide which two ocean animals and ocean plants they would like to research for their projects.

The students then complete their research and design their multimedia project using the *Multimedia/Slide Show Planning Sheet* (page 43). This helps them make certain design decisions ahead of time and keeps them from wasting time during their computer rotation.

Student partners need to have time to work together on their computer project. Once all the planning is done, the students should have approximately one month to complete their projects.

Oceanography Multimedia Projects *(cont.)*

The requirements the students have for this project are indicated on the *Student Assessment* sheets (pages 100–101). Have the students use the checklists to self-assess their projects before turning them in to the teacher.

After all the hard work, the students share their presentations with the rest of the class. Teachers can use the *Teacher Assessment* sheets (pages 98–99) to evaluate the students as they present.

Extension

Students can extend their research by comparing and contrasting their information about the ocean ecosystem to that of animals and plants in a lake or river ecosystem.

Student Names _____

Teacher Assessment Language Criteria

Language Criteria—(point value)   **Points Earned**

1. Title page has title and student names (5)   _____

2. All required information for the various topics is included in the project (15)   _____

3. Information is organized and in an appropriate sequence (10)   _____

4. Information is presented in the students' own words (10)   _____

5. Presentation and writing shows creativity (10)   _____

6. All information is in complete sentences (10)   _____

7. Spelling and capitalization are correct (10)   _____

8. Punctuation is correctly used (10)   _____

9. Effective word choice is demonstrated (5)   _____

10. All appropriate information is in the bibliography (5)   _____

11. Bibliography is in correct sequence and format (5)   _____

12. Project was completed on time (5)   _____

Total Points Earned   _____

Possible Points   **100**

Comments: _____

_____

_____

_____

Student Names _____

Teacher Assessment Technical Criteria

Technical Criteria—(point value)   **Points Earned**

1. Included at least one picture from the Internet (10)   _____

2. Included at least one color, scanned picture (10)   _____

3. Included at least one color picture from a digital camera (10)   _____

4. Included at least one imported song or music selection (10)   _____

5. Included at least one imported sound—voice or animal (10)   _____

6. Included at least one imported moving video (15)   _____

7. Included at least one clip art image (5)   _____

8. Included at least some animated text (5)   _____

9. All graphics coordinate with the topic (5)   _____

10. All slides/scenes/cards are linked in a logical order (5)   _____

11. All fonts are large enough and easy to read (10)   _____

12. Each slide/scene/card is neat and organized (5)   _____

Total Points Earned   _____

Possible Points   **100**

Comments: _____

_____

_____

_____

Names_____

Student Assessment Language Criteria

Did we check to make sure we completed the following language criteria?

- included a title page with the title and our names (5)   yes   no

- covered all information required for our various topics/subtopics (15)   yes   no

- organized information in an appropriate sequence (10)   yes   no

- given quality information in **our own words** (10)   yes   no

- showed creativity in our presentation and writing (10)   yes   no

- written all information using complete sentences (10)   yes   no

- checked our spelling and capitalization carefully (10)   yes   no

- checked our use of punctuation carefully (10)   yes   no

- used effective word choices (5)   yes   no

- included a bibliography with all appropriate information (5)   yes   no

- included a bibliography that is in the appropriate order (5)   yes   no

- completed the project on time (5)   yes   no

Our project is ready to be presented to the class!

Names_____

Student Assessment Technical Criteria

Have we included the following technical criteria?

- at least one picture from the Internet (10)   yes   no

- at least one color, scanned picture (10)   yes   no

- at least one color picture from a digital camera (10)   yes   no

- at least one imported song or music selection (10)   yes   no

- at least one imported sound—voice or animal (10)   yes   no

- at least one imported moving video (15)   yes   no

- at least one clip art image (5)   yes   no

- at least some animated text (5)   yes   no

- all graphics coordinate with the topic (5)   yes   no

- all slides/scenes/cards are in a logical order (5)   yes   no

- all fonts are large enough and easy to read (10)   yes   no

- each slide/scene/card is neat and organized (5)   yes   no

Our project is ready to be presented to the class!

The Body Electric

Objective

In this activity, students will

- create a multimedia encyclopedia about the human body.

Technology required

- *PowerPoint*, *HyperStudio*, *Scene Slate*, or another multimedia program
- scanner
- graphics of human body images

Materials needed

- photos or pictures of the human body

Description

Each student researches one of the body systems (i.e., circulatory or respiratory). Once their research is complete, the students need to find graphics of their systems. Each student can create one, scan one from print-resource materials, use a graphic from a CD-ROM, or download one from the Internet.

Using multimedia software, have the students place the graphics in presentations. If the software program has this capability, have students create invisible buttons to place over appropriate sections of the graphic. Link these buttons to new slides/scenes/cards that tell about that particular body part. These new slides/scenes/cards should also have graphics, appropriate videos, or a narrative that tells about each part. If the software program does not have button capability, have the students create a linear trip through their body systems. They can start at one part and give the class a virtual field trip through the system.

When finished, other students can look up information on different parts of the body system based on the research that other students have done. Each student, in effect, creates a reference volume on his/her particular body system.

Extension

This lesson could easily be adapted to almost any subject area requiring research. For example, you could do the same thing with a map of the United States where you click on a state to get information about it. It could also be done as an individual, group, or class project.

Weather Wizards

Objectives

In this activity, students will

- gather weather data daily using weather instruments, Internet sites, and the newspaper.
- e-mail weather pals daily to relay data back and forth about weather conditions.
- use a spreadsheet program with graphing capabilities to compile the data.

Technology required

- Internet connection
- e-mail access and account
- spreadsheet program
- printer

Materials needed

- daily newspapers
- weather instruments

Description

Online weather projects may already be underway in various places across the country, so teachers might want to look into joining an ongoing project. To find out more information and view some great collaborative projects, visit the *Global Schoolhouse* Web site. Access the site through the *Teacher Created Materials* Web site for this book.

> Go to **http://www.teachercreated.com/books/3032**
>
> Click on Page 103, Site 1

Some teachers might want to initiate their own projects rather than joining an ongoing project. Either way, before beginning, conduct lessons on weather concepts and weather measurement.

The data compiled by the students may include high and low temperatures, cloud type and percent coverage, humidity, air pressure, and precipitation. Have the students gather, record, and e-mail weather data on a consistent basis. As e-mail from other schools comes in, have the students record the data on charts.

Weather Wizards *(cont.)*

Teachers should consider using ePALS for free student e-mail accounts. Teachers are able to set up accounts for the students, monitor their students' outgoing mail, and keep track of passwords through this very teacher-friendly Web site. For more information, access the *ePALS* Web site through the *Teacher Created Materials* Web site for this book.

Go to **http://www.teachercreated.com/books/3032**

Click on Page 104, Site 1

Using a spreadsheet program with graphing capabilities, have the students enter and graph the data. Some of the graphs that can be made include: high and low temperatures over a period of weeks from one school; comparison graphs of data (temperature, barometric pressure, etc.) from two or more schools; and average high and low temperatures from all schools. Some example graphs are shown on pages 105–106.

Steps for Creating a Graph

1. Enter the data into a spreadsheet document as it is reported to the students.

2. Create a graph by following the directions provided by the spreadsheet program.

3. Select and copy the graph.

4. Open a draw or word processing document and paste the graph.

5. Rotate the page to landscape view.

6. Resize the graph to fill the page, leaving room for a header.

7. Make sure the graph has a title and all its labels.

8. Check to be sure the graph's key is accurate.

9. Print the graph on a color printer if possible.

Extension

Plot the locations of all the schools involved in the project on a map. Through e-mail messages, the class can get geographical information on the various locations. Write and mail postcards showing local views of each of the participating schools.

Weather Wizards Example

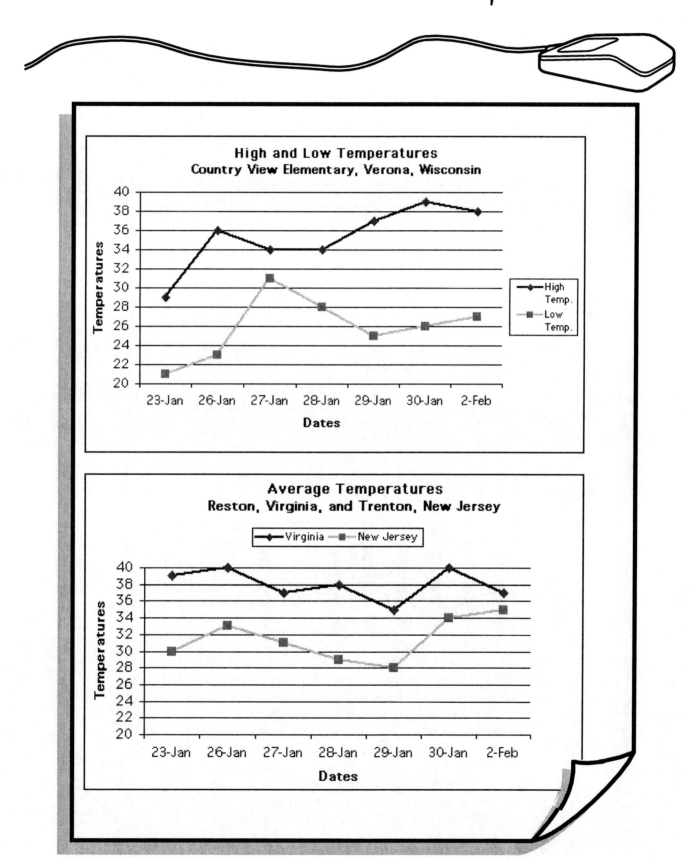

Weather Wizards Example (cont.)

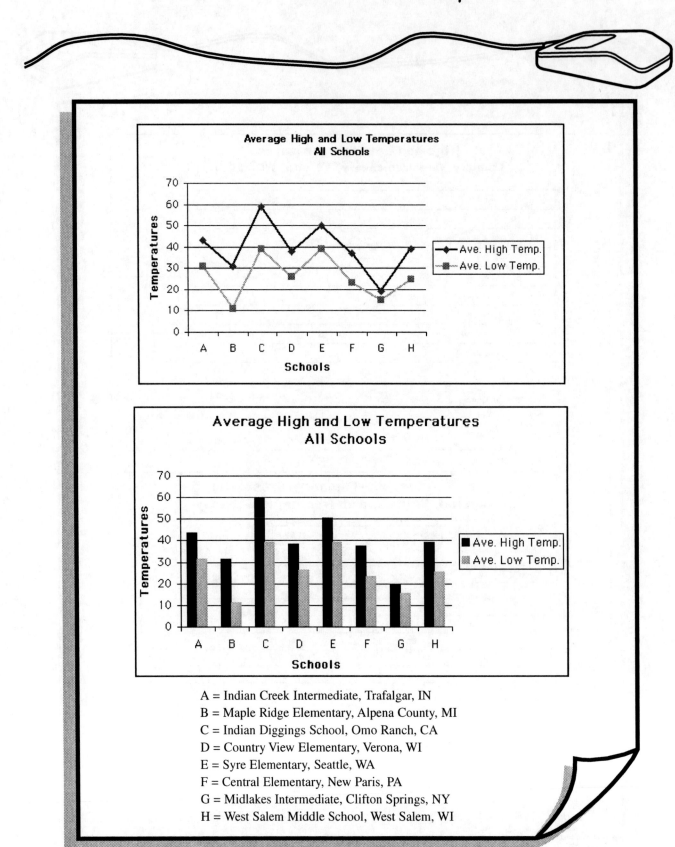

A = Indian Creek Intermediate, Trafalgar, IN
B = Maple Ridge Elementary, Alpena County, MI
C = Indian Diggings School, Omo Ranch, CA
D = Country View Elementary, Verona, WI
E = Syre Elementary, Seattle, WA
F = Central Elementary, New Paris, PA
G = Midlakes Intermediate, Clifton Springs, NY
H = West Salem Middle School, West Salem, WI

Countries of the World

Objectives

In this activity, students will

- use their research skills to learn about countries of their choice.
- use their understanding of a computer graphics program to create at least two slides.
- demonstrate their ability to save and retrieve information from their disks.

Technology required

- *Kid Pix* or other graphics program
- Internet connection
- printer

Materials needed

- world maps
- slide templates
- encyclopedias or other reference books
- copies of the *Countries Templates* sheets (pages 109–110) for the students

Description

Each student selects a country and then researches the following aspects about the country:

- the capital city
- the flag
- language(s) spoken
- the country's continent
- fun facts

Countries of the World *(cont.)*

After the students finish their initial research, have each student create two slides about his/her country. The first slide must name the country and illustrate the flag. The second slide shows the map outline of the country, lists the continent on which the country is located, and indicates where the capital is located. Finally, have the students draw pictures on their second slide that show what makes each country well known. Teachers can have the students plan their pages before going on the computer by using the *Countries Templates* activity sheets (pages 109–110).

Each student should have his or her own disk on which to save the created slides. The students should print copies of their slides so that the teacher can edit the slides.

The teacher should then provide a schedule for compiling the slides into one class slide show. Organize the students into small groups according to the continents where their countries are located, and then load the slides continent by continent.

As the students load their two slides, they can record their voices explaining what the slides depict and choose transitions between slides. Don't forget to view the entire slide show with the class!

Extension

This activity could be accelerated so that the students create more than two slides relating to their countries. A further modification would be to have the students create a slide for each of the seven continents. These could then serve as transitions between sections of the slide show. A student could also create a mini slide show of numerous slides highlighting a specific country.

Name _____

Countries Template

Slide #1

The country I researched was _____.

Here is the flag of the country I researched.

Name _____

Countries Template *(cont.)*

Slide #2

_____ is on the continent of _____.

Place a picture that shows your country's culture here.

Draw the outline of your country here. Put an x where the capital is located.

It is famous for _____, _____, and _____.

Learning About the Presidents

Objectives

In this activity, students will

- learn how to find pictures on the Internet.
- show their understanding and knowledge of the U.S. presidents.

Technology required

- Internet connection
- *Microsoft Word, AppleWorks*, or other word processing program
- printer

Materials needed

- pictures of the presidents (optional)

Description

The students will be creating informational cards about the country's presidents. The first step is for the teacher to assign each student a president to research. Teachers can either let the students pick their own presidents to research or the students can be assigned presidents.

Begin by showing students how to access the Internet Public Library's *Presidents of the United States* (*POTUS*) Web site through the *Teacher Created Materials* Web site for this book:

> Go to **http://www.teachercreated.com/books/3032**
>
> Click on Page 111, Site 1

Have each student use this Web site to locate a picture of the president he/she has been assigned. The student should use the page about his/her president to find pictures and information about the historic man. Each student should copy a picture or two to place in a word processing document. Then, the student should type facts about the president around his picture. Some teachers of kindergarten and first grade may want to complete this part as a class. When the students have enough facts around their pictures, they should print their documents.

Extension

Follow the same procedure for a famous person in African-American history, a famous woman in history, or a famous scientist.

Map Your Neighborhood

Objectives

In this activity, students will

- find their neighborhoods on a map.
- use the Internet to find information.

Technology required

- Internet connection
- printer

Materials needed

- students' addresses
- construction paper
- glue

Description

Each student needs to know his/her own address—house number, street name, and zip code.

Students begin by accessing the *MapQuest* Web site through the *Teacher Created Materials* Web site for this book:

> Go to **http://www.teachercreated.com/books/3032**
>
> Click on Page 112, Site 1

Have them click on the link for **Maps**.

Have the students fill in their addresses. When all the information has been completed, *MapQuest* will show maps of their neighborhoods with stars to indicate where their houses are located on the maps. In order to get a closer view of their neighborhoods, have the students click on the stars on their maps. Then, the students can copy their maps (click and hold on the map, drag to *copy this image*) and paste them into word processing files to print.

Once the students have printed their maps, have the students glue their maps on larger pieces of construction paper. They can then draw pictures of other neighborhood sites to complete their maps.

Extension

Have the students create brochures with the highlights of their neighborhoods.

Mt. Everest: The Highest Mountain in the World

Objectives

In this activity, students will

- use the Internet to learn about Mount Everest's flora, fauna, and folklore.
- review and apply knowledge of landforms.
- apply their imaginations and art skills to sketch a "yeti" from descriptions given on the Web site.

Technology required

- Internet connection

Materials needed

- copies of *Mt. Everest Facts* (page 114) for the students

Description

Students can work either independently or with partners, depending on computer availability and student ability to complete the activity page. This activity may be most appropriate for second grade classes.

Show students how to begin by accessing the *Mount Everest Homepage* through the *Teacher Created Materials* Web site for this book:

> Go to **http://www.teachercreated.com/books/3032**
>
> Click on Page 114, Site 1

On the Web site, the students will read and learn about the following main Mt. Everest topics:

- mountains and glaciers
- animals
- solar power
- Sherpas
- geography
- weather
- religion
- gear
- food

Extension

Student facilitators can hold class discussions. Require a fun fact from each of the main topics. Turn it into a compare/contrast lesson using other major world peaks (K2, Annapurna, etc.).

Name _____

Mt. Everest Facts

Read the *Mount Everest Homepage* to complete this page.

Go to **http://www.teachercreated.com/books/3032**
Click on Page 114, Site 1

Plants and Animals

1. Name two animals in the Mt. Everest region:_____

   _____

2. Name two plants in the Mt. Everest region: _____

   _____

Folklore

3. Write two yeti facts:

   • _____

   • _____

4. Sketch a yeti on the back of this paper.

Read and learn what you can from these main topics.

- mountains and glaciers
- animals
- solar power
- Sherpas
- geography
- weather
- religion
- gear
- food

5. Write five fun facts you learned about Mt. Everest:

   • _____

   • _____

   • _____

   • _____

   • _____

Where in the World Were You Born?

Objective

In this activity, students will

- tell and show, geographically, where they were born.

Technology required

- video camera
- digital camera
- *PowerPoint, HyperStudio, Scene Slate*, or another multimedia program

Materials needed

- world maps and/or globe
- U.S. map

Description

Take a digital photo of the class with a map in the background. Have the students find out where they were born (city, state, and country).

Videotape the students standing in front of the map. Have the students indicate where on the map they were born. They can point to the location as they talk about when and where they were born. Have the students share other interesting information about themselves as they are recorded.

Using a multimedia program, work with the students to develop slides/scenes/cards that connect each student's video clip to the class photo. If your multimedia program allows, make invisible buttons on each student's face. To view the finished product, click on the invisible button that is on each student's face in the class photo to go to the scene of the individual video of that student.

If your multimedia program does not have invisible buttons, have the students make a linear presentation where each student's video plays as someone proceeds through the presentation.

Extension

Students can present information on the state where they were born (i.e. capital, state flower, bird, and weather). Students can also graph the geographical areas where they were born.

World Map

Objectives

In this activity, students will

- apply their understanding of the continents and oceans.
- demonstrate their knowledge of north, south, east, and west.
- show that they can use a map to find the countries they are researching.

Technology required

- Internet connection

Materials needed

- copies of *Online World Map* (page 117) for the students
- world maps

Description

This activity is best if used as students are researching countries of their choice. If desired, teachers could choose one country and have the students complete the activity for the designated country. This activity should be done with buddies so that the students can help each other locate the seven continents.

A basic knowledge of the continents, oceans, equator, and cardinal compass directions is necessary. The students should know where the continents and oceans are located in relation to each other. They should be able to find the equator on a map and understand north, south, east, and west. If the class has not covered this information yet, this might be a good activity to complete as a whole group.

Have the students work with their buddies to complete the activity page. Before they go to the computer, show the students how to access the *Houghton Mifflin World Countries* Web site and the *Flags and Maps of the World* Web site through the *Teacher Created Materials* Web site for this book:

> Go to **http://www.teachercreated.com/books/3032**
>
> Click on Page 117, Site 1 and Site 2

The *Flags and Maps of the World* Web site gives the names of the countries and continents, so be sure the students begin on Site 1.

Extension

Students can design questions of their own to challenge their fellow students.

Online World Map

Go to the Houghton Mifflin *World Countries* Web site:

    Go to **http://www.teachercreated.com/books/3032**

    Click on Page 117, Site 1

Use this Web site and the one listed below to answer these questions with your buddy.

1. Show your buddy the seven continents by naming and pointing to each on the computer.

2. What country are you researching? _____

    Show your buddy where it is.

3. Look at the country you're researching and answer the following:

    • What country or ocean is to the north?   _____

    • What country or ocean is to the south?   _____

    • What country or ocean is to the east?   _____

    • What country or ocean is to the west?   _____

4. Name four countries that touch the equator:

    _____   _____

    _____   _____

5. What is the largest country in Asia? _____

6. What is the largest country in South America? _____

Challenges:

• Name three countries in Africa: _____

    _____

• What island is southeast of Australia? _____

> Also use the *Flags and Maps of the World* Web site to find these answers.
>
>   Go to **http://www.teachercreated.com/books/3032**
>
> Click on Page 117, Site 2

American Quilt

Objectives

In this activity, students will

- learn symbols of their state along with other special features about their state.
- learn facts about the other 49 states.

Technology required

- *Microsoft Word, AppleWorks*, or other word processing program
- *AppleWorks, Microsoft Works*, or other drawing program
- Internet connection
- e-mail access and account

Materials needed

- research materials
- copies of *Quilt Pattern Template* (page 120) for the students
- 50, 8" x 8" fabric squares and fabric scraps
- fabric paint
- needle and thread

Description

This lesson includes general information about individual states. Prior to the lesson, a contact person from each of the other 49 states should be established. If 49 contacts cannot be found, teachers should try to locate as many as possible so that their students will have less work. A good place to find teachers for collaboration is on the Internet. There are a few Web sites where teachers can present their project ideas and ask for volunteers from other states.

Two Web sites that teachers might want to check out are the *Global Schoolhouse* Web site and *Intercultural E-Mail Classroom Connections* (IECC). Access these sites through the *Teacher Created Materials* Web site for this book.

Go to **http://www.teachercreated.com/books/3032**

Click on Page 118, Site 1 or Site 2

American Quilt *(cont.)*

Teachers should consider using ePALS for free student e-mail accounts. Teachers are able to set up accounts for the students, monitor their students' outgoing mail, and keep track of passwords through this very teacher-friendly Web site. For more information, access the *ePALS* Web site through the *Teacher Created Materials* Web site for this book.

Go to **http://www.teachercreated.com/books/3032**

Click on Page 119, Site 1

To begin, the students need to learn about their own state. They should learn the symbols of their state along with other special features about their state. Using the *Quilt Pattern Template* (page 120) or a drawing program, they then design a quilt patch that shares this unique information about their state. The quilt patch should include information in both picture and word form.

The students then type an information sheet to accompany each square. The teacher may set up a template or allow each student to do his/her own composition. Once the squares are completed, the students e-mail their squares and the information sheets to the contact people (or their students) from the other 49 states. If the paper template page was used to design the squares, have the students scan their work into the computer and send the file as an attachment to an e-mail.

It is great fun to receive quilt designs from the other states and learn about each of their special features. As the designs arrive, have the students turn the designs into actual quilt squares using the fabric squares and fabric paint. When all 50 are in (don't forget to have a student make one from your home state), sew the squares together and display the quilts in your school.

Note: An alternative is to have the students from each state make the quilt squares and mail the quilt squares themselves to the 49 contacts around the country. This way may cost more in postage, but it alleviates the issue of setting up student e-mail accounts.

Extension

Each student may do a report on a state of his/her choice. All the students may study and learn the 50 states and capitals. Other quilts may be made using pattern blocks or other geometrical concepts.

Name _____

Quilt Pattern Template

Directions: Use the square below to design your quilt square. Be sure your work is very neat so that another student can understand it. Your one-page description should describe how all of the symbols on this quilt square relate to your home state.

Around the World in Pursuit of Mr. Big

Objectives

In this activity, students will

- use various technology tools (the Internet, a spreadsheet, and e-mail) to take a virtual trip around the world.
- learn about exchange rates, staying within a budget, and spending money wisely.

Technology required

- Internet connection with e-mail access and account
- spreadsheet program

Materials needed

- copies of *Daily Expense Report* (page 123) for the students
- calculators (optional)
- encyclopedias and other reference materials (electronic or text)

Description

Organize the students into groups of two to four. Tell them that they will be taking a virtual trip around the world in search of a fictitious character, Mr. Big, notorious international art thief. Mr. Big plays cat and mouse with his pursuers by sending them daily e-mail messages that offer clues as to where he is at the current time.

Teachers should consider using ePALS for free student e-mail accounts. Teachers are able to set up accounts for the students, monitor their students' outgoing mail, and keep track of passwords through this very teacher-friendly Web site. For more information, access the *ePALS* Web site through the *Teacher Created Materials* Web site for this book.

Go to **http://www.teachercreated.com/books/3032**

Click on Page 121, Site 1

Give the students a time frame within which they must capture Mr. Big (usually three to six weeks) and a budget for travel, hotels, meals, etc. ($10,000 is a good figure). Students then create a spreadsheet (with instruction and assistance as needed) which helps them keep track of expenses. The spreadsheet could also be set up in advance by the teacher so the students need only enter data. It should be set up in such a way as to subtract daily expenses automatically from the total budget provided.

Around the World in Pursuit of Mr. Big (cont.)

Each day, the students check their e-mail for a message from Mr. Big. The teacher acts as Mr. Big by sending messages. A separate e-mail account should be set up in advance with the user ID as "mrbig." Each day, Mr. Big gives them a set of clues, such as "I am in a location where people speak French, the food is delicious, and the Mona Lisa sits waiting to be stolen in the Louvre museum." Students research the clues and determine where he is (in this case, Paris). When they discover where he is located, the students must respond to his e-mail telling where they think he is located.

Students must then use the Internet to see how much a flight to Mr. Big's location would cost, the local currency, and the exchange rate so that they can calculate their expenses.

The *USA Today* business section posts daily exchange rates.

Go to **http://www.teachercreated.com/books/3032**

Click on page 122, Site 1

Some expenses can be standardized to make things a bit simpler. For example, $100 a night for a hotel, $75 a day for food, and $50 a day for miscellaneous expenses. They then fill out a *Daily Expense Report* (page 123) which they must submit to you. This page shows their expenses in U.S. dollars and the local currency. They enter the same information into their computer spreadsheets and note the balance left. They then mark their world maps with Mr. Big's current location and "fly there."

The following day, the procedure is repeated. Mr. Big moves to another location and the students once again research airfares, calculate expenses in the local currency, submit expense account forms, etc. Toward the end of the game, clues should be confined to one location (such as New York City) so that Mr. Big can be caught. This is when the game gets more challenging, since the clues force them to do more thorough research into a specific location. For example, if Mr. Big is in New York City, various daily clues could be offered for several locations in New York City (the Empire State Building, the World Trade Center, Times Square, etc.).

When the students catch Mr. Big, he e-mails them from jail with the message, "Curses! Foiled Again!"

Extension

Students can modify the spreadsheet so that it calculates the various exchange rates automatically. Students can also be given less money, which requires them to shop for cheaper airfares online. Clues could also rely more heavily on which works of art Mr. Big is interested in, which would require the students to learn more about them. Various art-related Internet sites are available to help the students accomplish this.

Daily Expense Report

Date: _____

Team Name: _____

Team Member Names: _____   _____

_____   _____

Traveling from _____ to _____.

	U.S. Dollars	Local Currency
Airfare		
Hotel		
Meals		
Miscellaneous		

Total amount left in your team's account: _____

Conflict with England

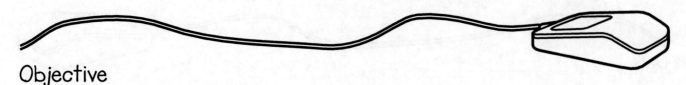

Objective

In this activity, students will

- create a multimedia project as the culmination of their study of the events of the American Revolution era.

Technology required

- *PowerPoint*, *HyperStudio*, *Scene Slate*, or another multimedia program
- Internet connection

Materials needed

- copies of *Multimedia/Slide Show Planning Sheet* (page 43) for the groups
- copies of *Group Project Guidelines* (page 125) for the groups
- copies of *Self and Partner Evaluation* (page 126) for the groups
- American Revolution research materials and images

Description

Put the students into groups of two. Give groups guidelines for their research which indicate what areas are to be covered. In general, they are required to focus on major issues and events during each of the following years: 1754, 1763, 1765, 1770, 1773, 1774, 1775, 1776, 1778, 1781, and 1783.

The students must complete note cards to prepare their research. They should have a separate card for each date on the time line with the date clearly written on each note card. They need to write complete and thorough notes on each event. Be sure they properly record the sources used on each note card.

Give the class a time line for the project. The students do their research and design the actual project format. The project must include a title page, a bibliography, a table of contents, and eleven slides/scenes/cards (one for each year). It must also include a graphic downloaded from the Internet, graphic imported from a clip art, at least two scanned graphics, text, an animated graphic, sound, and a digitized movie. Have the students use the *Multimedia/Slide Show Planning Sheet* (page 43) to plan their presentations.

Students should use the *Group Project Guidelines* (page 125) as a checklist while they complete the project. The *Self and Partner Evaluation* (page 126) makes a nice assessment after the project is completed.

Extension

Students can extend their research into areas that especially interest them. They can also stretch the technological boundaries by including more scanned images or integrating digital movies more fully.

Group Project Guidelines

Directions: Use this checklist as a guideline for things to be included in your multimedia project. Keep in mind that these are only the minimum requirements.

_____ title page
_____ bibliography page
_____ sound on at least two different slides/scenes/cards
_____ at least one graphic downloaded from the Internet
_____ at least one graphic imported from clip art
_____ at least one scanned photo
_____ at least one animated graphic
_____ at least one movie

A slide/scene/card for each of the following years:

_____ 1754		_____ 1773		_____ 1778	
_____ 1763		_____ 1774		_____ 1781	
_____ 1765		_____ 1775		_____ 1783	
_____ 1770		_____ 1776			

Note Cards

_____ a separate card for each date on the time line
_____ the time line date clearly written on each note card
_____ complete and thorough notes on each event
_____ properly recorded the sources used on each note card
_____ names are on the note cards

Multimedia Planning Sheet

_____ a slide/scene/card planned for every event
_____ chosen and noted the graphics to use for each slide/scene/card
_____ written down exactly where to find the graphics
_____ planned what to use for our movies
_____ planned the sounds and on which slides/scenes/cards to use them

Name_____ Partner's Name _____

Self and Partner Evaluation

I was prepared and had my materials when my partner and I worked.	always	most of the time	sometimes	rarely
I was responsible for getting my share of our work completed on time.	always	most of the time	sometimes	rarely
I was organized and kept track of all things for which I was responsible.	always	most of the time	sometimes	rarely
I contributed ideas.	always	most of the time	sometimes	rarely
I listened to my partner's ideas.	always	most of the time	sometimes	rarely
I was willing to compromise.	always	most of the time	sometimes	rarely
I made sure my work reflected my best effort by taking my time and being careful.	always	most of the time	sometimes	rarely
I created my share of the slides/scenes/cards.	always	most of the time	sometimes	rarely
I actively participated in the development of our project.	always	most of the time	sometimes	rarely

My partner was prepared and had his/her materials when we worked.	always	most of the time	sometimes	rarely
My partner was responsible for getting his/her share of our work completed on time.	always	most of the time	sometimes	rarely
My partner was organized and kept track of all things for which he/she was responsible.	always	most of the time	sometimes	rarely
My partner contributed ideas.	always	most of the time	sometimes	rarely
My partner listened to my ideas.	always	most of the time	sometimes	rarely
My partner was willing to compromise.	always	most of the time	sometimes	rarely
My partner did his/her best work by taking time and being careful.	always	most of the time	sometimes	rarely
My partner created his/her share of scenes/slides/cards.	always	most of the time	sometimes	rarely
My partner actively participated in the development of our project.	always	most of the time	sometimes	rarely

Holiday Customs Around the World

Objective

In this activity, students will

- learn and share their knowledge of the customs of December holidays from around the world.

Technology required

- *PowerPoint, HyperStudio, Scene Slate,* or another multimedia program
- Internet connection

Materials needed

- books and magazines
- interviews with people from selected countries

Description

Ask the students to research holiday customs from various countries. Have them gather pictures of their countries' flags, basic customs, and foods. Each student should write a narrative that tells about how the holiday custom came to be celebrated in that country.

After the students complete their research, they must create a multimedia presentation to share their knowledge. The presentation is meant to tell the story of the holiday traditions in each country. The slides should feed seamlessly into each other with the student as the storyteller through the pictures and words on the slide. Their presentation should include a minimum of five slides/scenes/cards.

The following are the technical requirements for their presentation: at least one scanned image; at least one computer-generated (student-drawn) image; at least one image downloaded from the Internet; at least one downloaded movie; and at least one slide/scene/card must also contain sound.

Once all the information is entered, the students will orally present their holiday celebration reports to the class. The reports can culminate with a sample of the foods that are usually eaten at this holiday time in their selected countries.

Extension

Dioramas, posters, or plays may be added to enhance the presentations. Consider having speakers come to discuss the customs and share experiences.

Maya Adventure

Objectives

In this activity, students will

- use a Web site to find pictures of traditional Mayan temples in the ancient cities of Tikal and Uxmal.
- compare the architecture: shapes, color of stone, and special designs of various ancient buildings.

Technology required

- *AppleWorks*, *Microsoft Works*, or other drawing program
- Internet connection

Materials needed

- copies of *Maya Adventure Online* (page 129) for the students

Description

This assignment combines using the Internet and a draw program to learn more about Mayan temples and architecture. This activity will help the students learn how to follow directions, how to go between different programs smoothly, and also how to easily combine writing and art in the same document.

Use this assignment after studying about the Mayans. Students follow the directions on the *Maya Adventure Online* (page 129) to complete this assignment. An example is provided on page 130. They may need to use a map of the Mayan cities to help them find the correct cities on the Internet site.

Show students how to begin by accessing the *Maya Adventure* Web site through the *Teacher Created Materials* Web site for this book:

> Go to **http://www.teachercreated.com/books/3032**

> Click on Page 129, Site 1

The students will compare and contrast the different types of temples they find in Tikal and Uxmal. They must write five descriptive sentences about the different architecture. Then, they draw their own pyramids, and write a paragraph explaining the uses of temples. All of the pictures, writing, and drawing should be in the same document.

Extension

Students can extend their research to comparing and contrasting the architecture and ceremonies of the Maya, Aztec, and Inca.

Name _____

Maya Adventure Online

Access the *Maya Adventure* Web site:

> Go to **http://www.teachercreated.com/books/3032**
> Click on Page 129, Site 1

Click on Start Your Adventure.

- Figure out which **X** is Tikal and click on it. Copy an image of *Temple 1* from the page. Remember what its name was so you can correctly label it in your new document.

- Minimize the browser window and open your drawing program.

- Paste your picture into your drawing document and toggle back (return) to your browser.

- Choose one other picture from Tikal and copy that image. (Be sure to label the name of that temple or building, too.)

- Paste that image into your drawing document.

Return to the browser and click on **Maya Sites**.

- Click on the **X** for Uxmal. Copy the image of the *Pyramid of the Magician* and paste it in the drawing document. Choose one more picture and paste it.

Now, quit the Internet browser.

1. Compare the architecture (shapes, color of stone, special designs, etc.) of the buildings in the two cities.

2. Use the text tool to write at least five descriptive sentences comparing the pyramids of Takal to those of Uxmal.

3. Finally, create your own pyramid or temple. Write a paragraph explaining the types of Mayan ceremonies you would celebrate in your temple. Be accurate to Mayan history.

Maya Adventure Example

1. The Tikal temple has a mound over the door, and the Uxmal one doesn't.

2. The Uxmal temple has very wide steps, and the Tixal temple's are tall and skinny.

3. The Tikal temple is tall and skinny, and the Uxmal temple is short and fat.

4. The Uxmal and the Tikal temples both have blocks leading up to the top of the temples.

5. The stone color of the Tikal Temple is white, and the stone color of the Uxmal temple is tan.

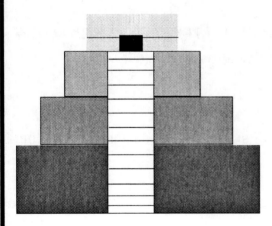

In my temple, we would do such ceremonies as praying for good crops and praying for victory in a battle. It would be where the priests would live and preach.

Native American Slide Show

Objectives

In this activity, students will

- gather information on Native American tribes.
- design slide shows to share the information on the tribe.

Technology required

- *PowerPoint, HyperStudio, Scene Slate,* or another multimedia program
- Internet connection
- scanner

Materials needed

- copies of the *Slide Show Planning Sheet* (page 132) for the students
- copies of the *Slide Show Evaluation* (page 133) for the students and teacher
- Native American reference books and pictures

Description

For this project, the students will be making a slide show about information they have gathered on Native American tribes. To add some increased technology skills to this project, the students have to create their slides using word processing, drawing, and graphics programs. Their slide shows will consist of a minimum of five slides, complete with text, graphics, and sound.

After studying the Native American people, the students begin to make rough drafts of their slides by using picture books and their knowledge of one tribe. Have the students use the *Slide Show Planning Sheet* (page 132) to plan their presentations. When the rough drafts are completed, have the students type each slide's text into a word processing program.

Next, they must prepare their graphics by either scanning in pictures, downloading pictures from the Internet, or creating their own pictures in *Kid Pix* or another graphics program.

Finally, the students open the multimedia program with slide show capabilities and copy their text and graphics onto the correct slides. When all five slides are complete, the students put them into a slide show, adding sound and slide transitions.

The *Slide Show Evaluation* sheet (page 133) can be used in two important ways. First, the students should receive copies of it as they begin the project so they can see how they will be evaluated. Then, the teacher can use the rubric to assess their projects when the students present.

Extension

Have the students add more slides to their shows or copy movies from the Internet or CD-ROMs onto their slides.

Name _____

Slide Show Planning Sheet

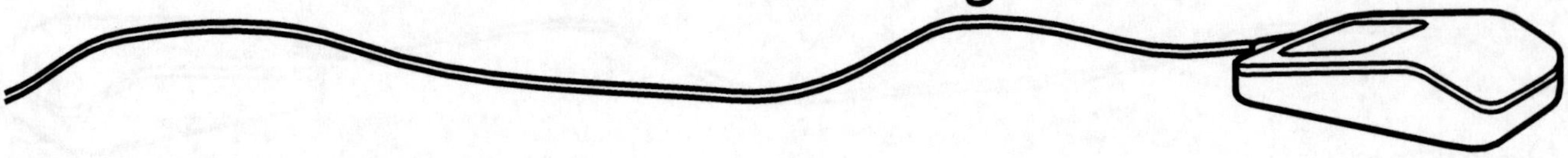

Plan for slide number _____

My text will say:

_____

_____

_____

_____

Here is a sketch of my picture:

The source for my picture is: _____

Other things I am adding are:

_____

_____

_____

Name _____

Slide Show Evaluation

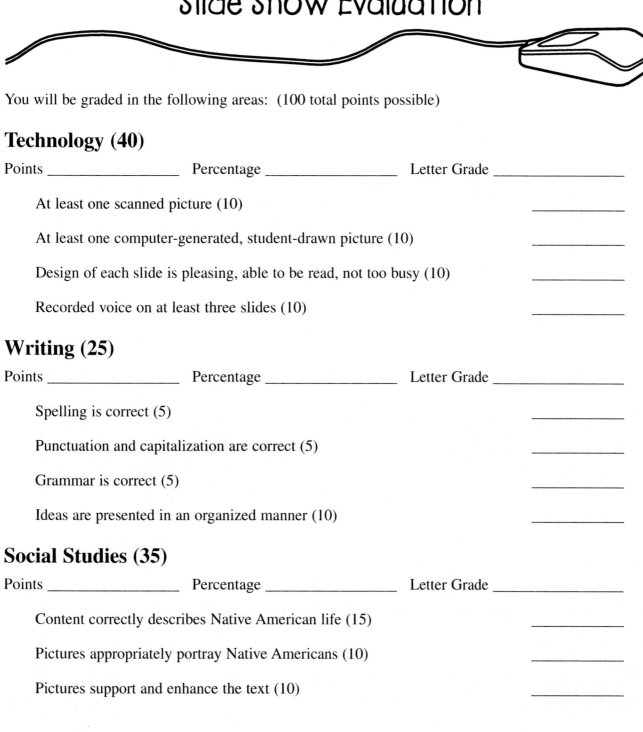

You will be graded in the following areas: (100 total points possible)

Technology (40)

Points _____ Percentage _____ Letter Grade _____

At least one scanned picture (10)   _____

At least one computer-generated, student-drawn picture (10)   _____

Design of each slide is pleasing, able to be read, not too busy (10)   _____

Recorded voice on at least three slides (10)   _____

Writing (25)

Points _____ Percentage _____ Letter Grade _____

Spelling is correct (5)   _____

Punctuation and capitalization are correct (5)   _____

Grammar is correct (5)   _____

Ideas are presented in an organized manner (10)   _____

Social Studies (35)

Points _____ Percentage _____ Letter Grade _____

Content correctly describes Native American life (15)   _____

Pictures appropriately portray Native Americans (10)   _____

Pictures support and enhance the text (10)   _____

Total Points (100)

Percentage _____   **Letter Grade** _____

Travel Brochures

Objective

In this activity, students will

• select points of interest in their state and produce travel brochures to advertise the locations.

Technology required

• *AppleWorks*, *Microsoft Works*, or other drawing program
• Internet connection
• scanner
• printer (preferably color)

Materials needed

• research materials

Description

The teacher should make a template in a draw program and save it as stationery. The template should resemble a tri-fold travel brochure. The students will open the template to complete this lesson.

The students gather information on various points of interest in their own state. Students should use print resource materials as well as state Web sites. Their information should include the sites' locations and information typically found in tourist brochures. After collecting the information, the students will type the key notes into the brochure template. Their writing needs to include interesting adjectives they have selected to describe their particular points of interest.

The next step is to locate pictures that highlight the point of interest and a map to show the location. These items can be scanned from a book or downloaded from the Internet. An example of a completed brochure is provided on page 135.

To produce the back of the brochure, reverse the template and use it again. The two sides are then printed in color, if possible, and glued together.

Extension

This activity may be extended to an overview of the 50 states by allowing each student to pick two states and do similar research to create brochures of the states, including size, location (with map), population, capital, and state symbols.

Travel Brochures Example

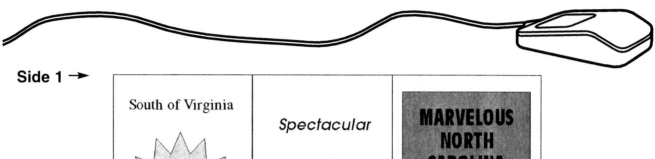

Side 1 →

South of Virginia

The Tar Heel State

North of
South Carolina

Spectacular

Awesome

Marvelous

Visit
North
Carolina

**MARVELOUS
NORTH
CAROLINA**

**Made by
Kelsi Smithers**

Side 2
↓

North
Carolina

North Carolina is a wonderful state
to visit because it is so historical
and beautiful. The state flower is
the glorious dogwood. The bright
cardinal is this southern state's
bird. The pine tree is the
magnificent tree of this coastal
state.

The capital of North Carolina is
Raleigh. The capital became a city
in 1791. New Bern was the capital
from 1771 to 1776. The largest
city in the large state is spectacular
Charlotte.

The beautiful state song is "Old
North State." Do you want to
know the state motto? "To be
rather than to seem."

The population is 7,070,000!!
Wow! The nickname is the Tar
Heel State. Don't miss this
exciting and historic state.

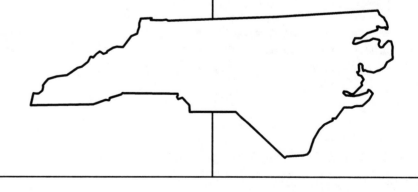

United States Constitution

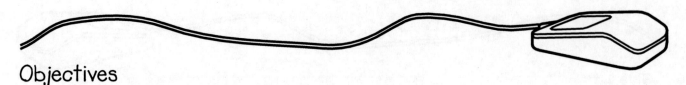

Objectives

In this activity, students will

- use a Web site to research who wrote the United States Constitution.
- learn what the Bill of Rights means to Americans.

Technology required

- *Microsoft Word, AppleWorks*, or other word processing program
- Internet connection

Materials needed

- copies of the *Internet Research* sheet (page 137) for the students

Description

This assignment has the students using the Internet to learn about the *U.S. Constitution*. This lesson should be completed after an introductory lesson about the Constitution and specifically, *The Bill of Rights*.

The students follow the instructions on the *Internet Research* activity sheet (page 137). Teachers may have the students work on this independently or in pairs. The students should write their answers on the activity page, or they may use a word processing program to record their answers.

On page 138, there is a sample of the drawing students are asked to complete. If the students do not understand the assignment, teachers might want to share the example drawing to give the students ideas of how to portray the signing of the Constitution.

Extension

Students can extend their research by comparing the *U.S. Constitution* to constitutions of other governments or by comparing it to other U.S. documents, such as the *Declaration of Independence* and *Articles of Confederation*.

Name _____

Internet Research

Access the *U.S. Constitution—Table of Articles* Web site:

> Go to **http://www.teachercreated.com/books/3032**

> Click on Page 137, Site 1

Click on the link for **Signers** and answer the following questions:

1. What year was the Constitution signed? _____

2. How many years after the United States declared its independence was this document signed? _____

3. Write yes or no to indicate if each of the following people signed the Constitution:

    a. James Madison _____

    b. Thomas Jefferson _____

    c. George Washington _____

    d. Alexander Hamilton _____

    e. Benjamin Franklin _____

4. Draw a picture of Congress signing the Constitution using a computer draw program. Be sure to label where this took place and label the different politicians who attended the ratification of the Constitution.

Click the **Back** button on your browser menu. When you return to the main page, click the link for **Amendments**. Click on **Amendment I** and then use the **Next Amendment** button to proceed through these changes to the Constitution.

5. As you read, decide which amendments give us the following rights:

    a. The right not to have cruel and unusual punishment _____

    b. The right not to testify against ourselves in court _____

    c. The right to own guns _____

    d. The right to protest nonviolently _____

    e. Our right to NOT have the government house troops in our homes during a time of war _____

    f. The right to a fair and speedy trial _____

    g. The right to be whatever religion we want _____

    h. The right to print documents that speak out for or against political issues _____

United States Constitution Example

Westward, Ho!

Objectives

In this activity, students will

- conduct research about the pioneers' movement West.
- create personal journals describing their own experiences.
- include graphics found on the Internet in their journals.

Technology required

- *PowerPoint, HyperStudio, Scene Slate,* or another multimedia program
- Internet connection

Materials needed

- none

Description

After a unit of study on the American Westward Movement, teachers can use this project as a means of assessing student knowledge. The students will create an electronic journal of a pioneer on a trail across America. They must play the role of a member of a pioneer family moving West.

In their journals, they must include a variety of information about their travels which will give others an idea of what pioneers went through on their journey across this rugged country.

Students must include multiple photographs or other digital images where appropriate. The journals can take any form but should be self-explanatory to someone who wants to view the presentation. So, any verbal descriptions should be recorded onto the slides. The students should be encouraged to include movies, pictures, trails, maps, and artifact descriptions.

Extension

Use this idea as an end of the year technology project. Have the students create journals that show all the incredible things they learned in the class this year. They can scan in pieces of their work and produce an electronic portfolio.

Glossary of Technology Terms

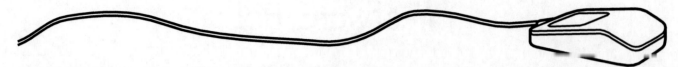

Following are some terms listed in this book as well as other commonly used technology terms. Although not comprehensive by any means, we thought it might benefit you to have some of the terms defined.

AppleWorks/ClarisWorks—is an integrated software program including word processing, database, spreadsheet, drawing, graphics, and presentation modules.

Bailey's Book House—is a card making program.

Browser—is a program, such as *Internet Explorer* or *Netscape Navigator*, which allows you to investigate Web sites on the Internet.

Button—is an icon that resembles a clickable object.

Cards—are pages in a multimedia project. These can also be called slides or scenes.

Cell—is the place where information is held in a spreadsheet.

Cell address—is the exact location of a specific cell. It is formed by noting the intersection of the column and row.

Center align—is to center words in the middle of the page. The words will be evenly spaced from the left and right margins.

Click—is to depress a button on the top of the mouse.

Clip art—is pre-drawn digital art for inclusion in documents or other presentations.

Clipboard—is a location inside the computer where items that have been selected are temporarily stored. Information remains on the clipboard until something new is placed there or the computer is shut down.

Close—is a menu item that puts away a file you are no longer using.

Columns—are the vertical spaces in a spreadsheet. Columns are headed with letters.

Computer rotation—is a cycle whereby students are ensured equitable computer time in a classroom where there are fewer computers than the students.

Copy—is to select text and place it on an internal clipboard to be placed elsewhere. The original text remains on the screen.

Cursor—is a blinking line or box that indicates where typed text will appear.

Cut—is to select text and place it on an internal clipboard to be placed elsewhere. The original text disappears from the screen.

Databases—are like electronic index card files. Imagine placing vital information about each student on an index card inside your computer, then asking your computer for the name and phone number of each student who has been in your school for one year or less. Instantly, you have a listing of all parents to whom you want to extend a personal welcome.

Digital camera—is a camera that takes pictures digitally, as opposed to using film.

Digital image—is an image that has been digitized or otherwise electronically manipulated.

Glossary of Technology Terms *(cont.)*

Digitized pictures—are pictures converted to digital language so that they can be displayed on a computer.

Digitized video—is video converted to digital language so that it can be displayed on a computer.

Double-click—is two, quick clicks on the mouse button.

Dragging—is the process of moving the mouse while holding the mouse button down. Dragging is used when text is being highlighted or a pulldown menu is in use. Objects are moved by dragging them.

Drawing tools—allow you to select the tools with which you will draw.

E-mail (electronic mail)—is a system where people send and receive messages through their computers on a network or using modems.

Enter/Return—sends the cursor to a new line. Pressing enter/return will make a selection.

Fields—are in a database. This is a separate category where information is entered.

File—is a document stored in the computer.

Filename—is the label (name) a file has been given.

Formula—is a string of commands used in a spreadsheet to add, subtract, average, and otherwise calculate a series of numbers automatically.

Graph—is a picture that shows data by using bars, lines, or symbols.

Graphics programs—are drawing or painting programs. A drawing program allows you to experiment with lines and shapes, forming individual items. A painting program gives you a blank canvas on which to create.

Highlight—is to drag the mouse over text to select it. A dark bar appears, indicating that the text is highlighted and ready to be manipulated.

HyperStudio—is a non-linear multimedia presentation similar to *PowerPoint* or *Scene Slate*.

Icon—is a small picture or image that represents a specific function.

Import/Insert—places text or graphics within your document.

Internet—is the largest system of interconnected networks of computers in the world. Among other functions, the Internet is used to connect to Web pages and send and receive e-mail.

Internet Explorer—is a program to browse the Internet.

Kid Pix—is a multimedia software program for younger students that integrates drawing and sound, stamps, and even QuickTime movies.

Landscape—is selecting horizontal orientation as opposed to vertical orientation when printing. The image prints sideways—11" x 8 1/2".

Linear—is a program in which navigational choices are limited to what comes before or after the current screen.

Glossary of Technology Terms *(cont.)*

Media—is the means of transmission of information, whether auditory, visual, or tactile.

Menu bar—is the listing on the top of the desktop. The pulldown menus are located here.

Microsoft Word—is a word processing and desktop publishing program.

Microsoft Works—is an integrated software program including word processing, database, and spreadsheet modules.

Minimize—is to shrink the open window so that you can use other programs. There is usually a button on the top bar of a window that will let you minimize it.

Monitors—are high-resolution display screens.

Mouse—is a small device that rolls on the table. It controls the selection and placement of items.

Multimedia presentation—is a presentation involving multiple forms of media, such as text, video, graphics, animation, and sound. Multimedia is to use, involve, or encompass several media or a combination of various forms of media. Special effects add to the total impact of showing material through this medium.

Navigation—is the process of moving through a program or project.

Netscape Navigator—is a program to browse the Internet.

Network—is a number of computers and other devices that are linked together so that they can share information and equipment.

Non-linear—indicates a program in which the user has a variety of navigational choices on a particular screen.

Online—means to be connected to a network.

PageMill—is Web design software.

Paste—is a menu item that places an item from the clipboard into a document.

Place—is putting text or graphics within your document.

Portrait—is selecting vertical orientation as opposed to horizontal orientation when printing. The image prints vertically—8 ½" x 11".

PowerPoint—is a multimedia presentation program similar to *HyperStudio* or *Scene Slate*.

Pulldown menu—is a list of choices that appear when a menu bar item has been clicked. Hold the mouse key down to read the pulldown menu.

QuickCam—is a brand of camera capable of sending video or still pictures over a network. Used for video conferencing.

Row—is a horizontal group of cells in a spreadsheet. Rows are named with numbers.

Scan/Scanner—is a device for digitizing photographs or images for display on a computer or inclusion in a computer document.

Glossary of Technology Terms *(cont.)*

Scanned image—is taking a photograph of a picture or other image for display on a computer or for insertion into computer documents.

Scene Slate—is a multimedia software program, similar to *PowerPoint* or *HyperStudio*.

Scenes—are each page of a multimedia project. These can be called slides or cards.

Select—is to choose an item. Graphics are selected by clicking on them, and text is selected by dragging the mouse over the words.

Slide show—is a multimedia presentation where each "slide" is a picture or page in a word processing document. When in slide show mode, each picture or page is displayed one at a time.

Slides—are each page of a multimedia project. These can be called scenes or cards.

Software—are programs that enable computers to carry out certain tasks.

Spreadsheet—is a program that gives you an electronic ledger for crunching numbers. How much money will your class have to raise in order to take that special class trip? What is the average of all math test scores for each student in your class? These questions can be answered using a spreadsheet program.

Stamp—is a tool used in some elementary graphics programs to place clip art pictures onto a blank page.

Stanley's Sticker Stories—is a program that helps students add graphics to their stories.

Stationery—is an item saved in a format which can be used over and over as a template.

Storyboard—is a series of panels or descriptions depicting the content and order of a multimedia presentation, story, or book.

Surfing—is to explore the Internet by jumping from one site to another.

Template—is a layout designed to be used over and over. (See stationery.)

Toggle—is to jump back and forth between two or more programs. Usually, you will minimize a program to open a new program and then toggle back to the first program.

Transitions—are the special effects used when moving from one slide/scene/card to another.

Video conferencing—is using a computer-compatible camera to communicate visually and through sound over a network.

Web site—is a collection of Web pages run by one person or organization.

Window—is the page that appears on the screen where your work is displayed or information is presented.

Word processing—is a program used to type something. Letters, tests, stories, review sheets, memos, and newsletters are examples of things for which a word processing program would be used.

Bibliography

Arachnology-Araneae,
**http://www.ufsia.ac.be/Arachnology/Pages/
Araneae.html**, 1995, Herman Vanuytven

Bailey's Book House, 1992–1995, used by permission of
Edmark Corporation, 1997

AppleWorks/ClarisWorks 4.0, 1993, 1994.
AppleWorks/ClarisWorks is a registered trademark of
Apple Computer, Inc.

CU-See-Me Video/Software, 0.8763 (PPC), 1993–1997,
Cornell University

Dinosaur Ridge, **http://www.dinoridge.org**, 1996,
Friends of Dinosaur Ridge

Discovery,
http://www.discovery.com/exp/spiders/upclose.html,
1998, Discovery Communication, Inc.

Flags and Maps of the World,
http://www.plcmc.lib.nc.us/kids/mow/, Public Library
of Charlotte & Mecklenburg County

Earth and Moon Viewer,
http://www.fourmilab.ch/earthview/vplanet.html,
1994, John Walker

Earth and Sky Home Page,
http://www.earthsky.com, Earth and Sky Radio series is
a production of EarthTalk, Inc., a 501(c)(3) organization,
719 Patterson Ave., Austin, TX 78703,
people@earthsky.com

Flashcards for Kids, **http://www.edu4kids.com/math/**,
1997, 1998, Infobahn Xpress

Global Schoolhouse, **http://www.gsn.org/**

WebMuseum: Gogh, Vincent van,
http://metalab.unc.edu/wm/paint/auth/gogh, 1996,
Nicolas Pioch

Internet Public Library,
**http://www.ipl.org/youth/StoryHour/spiders/
cover.html**, Internet Public Library, Ann Arbor, MI

Kid Pix 2.0, 1994, Craig Hickman and Broderbund (The
Learning Company)

Mapquest, **http://www.mapquest.com**

Maya Adventure, **http://www.smm.org/sln/ma/**, 1999,
Science Museum of Minnesota

Meet the Corals,
http://www.FisheyeView.com/FVCam.html, 1997,
Quantum Leap Network, Inc., 1995-99 Rob and Robin
Burr, Box 144353 Coral Gables, FL 33114,
comments@FisheyeView.com

Mount Everest Home Page,
**http://www.newton.mec.edu/angier/Ferguson/Everest/
home.html**, 1998, Ask Fergie

PageMill 2.0 & 3.0, Adobe and PageMill are trademarks
of the Adobe Systems, Inc., 1996

QuickCam Software 2.1, 1996, Connectix Corporation

Sammy's Science House, 1994, used by permission of
Edmark, 1997.

Scene Slate, 1995, Learning Systems Consultants, Inc.,
1995. All rights reserved.

Science Museum of Minnesota,
**http://www.smm.org/sln/tf/s/segment/segment.html,
http://www.smm.org/sln/tf/books/bugs.html**, 1995

Sea World's Coral and Coral Reefs,
http://www.seaworld.org/coral_reefs/introcr.html,
1999, Sea World/Busch Gardens Animal Information
Database, Sea World, Inc.

Stanley's Sticker Stories, 1996, used by permission of
Edmark, 1997

Tarantulas, **http://www.petsnus.com/trantual.htm**

The Bug Jester,
http://members.aol.com/YESedu/jester.html, Young
Entomologists Society, Lansing, MI

TesselMania!, MECC (The Learning Company), 1994

University of Kentucky Entomology for Kids,
**http://www.uky.edu/Agriculture/Entomology/ythfacts/
bugfood/bugfood1.htm**,
**http://www.uky.edu/Agriculture/Entomology/ythfacts/
stories/hurtrnot.htm**, 1997

USA Today, **http://www.usatoday.com/**

Virtual Body, **http://www.ehc.com/vbody.asp**, EHC.com

World Countries,
http://www.eduplace.com/ss/ssmaps/wrldcoun.html,
1998, Houghton Mifflin Company

Note: These Web sites and software editions valid as of
publication.